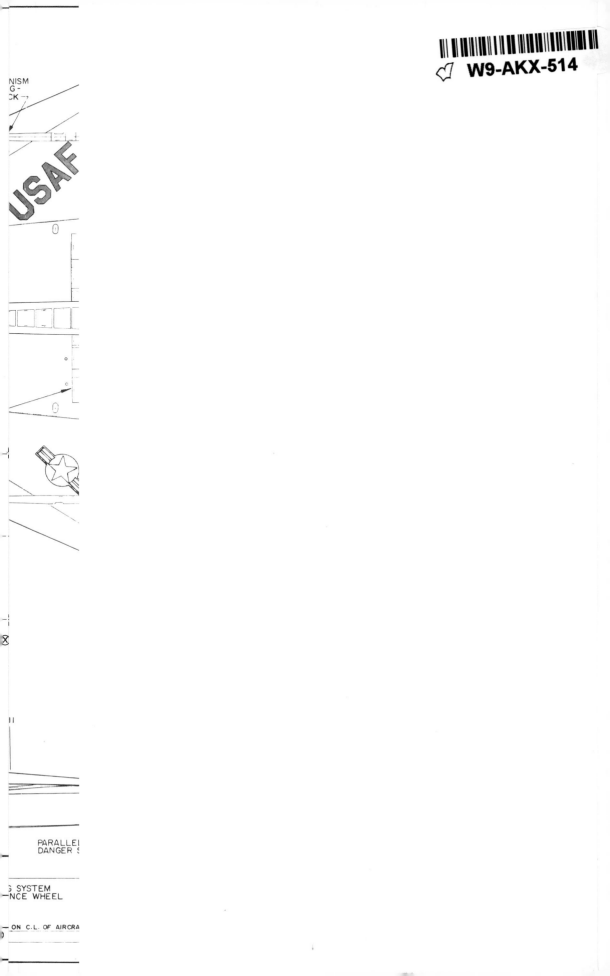

AERO SERIES VOL. 30

NORTH AMERICAN
VALKYRIE
XB-70A

STEVE PACE

AERO
A division of TAB BOOKS Inc.
Blue Ridge Summit, PA 17214

FIRST EDITION

THIRD PRINTING

Printed in the United States of America

Reproduction or publication of the content in any manner, without express
permission of the publisher, is prohibited. No liability is assumed with respect to
the use of the information herein.

Library of Congress Cataloging in Publication Data

Pace, Steve.
North American Valkyrie XB-70A.

(Aero series; vol. 30)
Bibliography: p.
Includes index.
1. B-70 bomber. I. Title.
UG1242.B6P33   1984   348.4'2   84-6450
ISBN 0-8168-0610-1

IN MEMORY OF MY MOTHER

ACKNOWLEDGMENTS

More than eight years were spent researching the North American XB-70. During that time many unselfish individuals helped with their contributions. Some contributed more than others. But even the smallest contribution was of great value. Each and every contribution was required to complete this volume of the Aero Series.

At this time I would like to acknowledge a few chief contributors which include: firstly, Gene Boswell, Public Relations Office at Rockwell International, who, now retired, offered his invaluable help from day one, who opened the door; secondly, Dr. Richard L. Schleicher of North American Aviation, Inc. (now Rockwell International, North American Aircraft Division), who, now retired, helped greatly with his vast knowledge of B-70 structures; thirdly, J. T. (Ted) Bear of the Edwards AFB History Office, who, now retired, supplied me with rare photographs, filling a void; fourthly, Douglas L. Emmons of Meta Model, who provided me with contacts, photos and data; and Paul Dawson of the General Electric Company, who has forgotten more about jet engines than I'll ever know.

I want to thank each and every contributor who helped me with the B-70 project. Those not previously mentioned are listed below. Hopefully, no one has been missed.

"Buzz" Holland	Gordon Williams
Harl Brackin	Harry Gann
Charles Worman	Paul Matt
Paul Spitzer	Robert Kemp
Lloyd Jones	Dick Seely
Lonna Brooks	E. H. Kolcum
Jim Gallagher	Douglas Pirus
Bob Morrison	Dominick Pisano
Ralph Jackson	Vincent Murone
Rob Mack	Al Misenko

INTRODUCTION

The North American XB-70A has been called a Pterodactyl for its flapping wingtips; The Great White Bird, for its beauty; The Thing for its monstrous size; Cecil, for its resemblance to TV's Seasick Sea Serpent; and the Valkyrie, for its decisive destructive potential incorporated in such beautiful form.

In 1954, the United States Air Force prompted the American aircraft industry to bring into being an advanced bomber for the Strategic Air Command. Ten years later the bomber flew, and what transpired from the XB-70A's inception to the time it left the ground makes a fascinating story.

The XB-70A Valkyrie became a legend in its own time. Its conception gave birth to advanced engineering, tooling, fabrication, metallurgy and construction processes. The challenge provided by the B-70 proved both extraordinary and unmatched throughout the latter half of the '50s and beginning of the '60s. Intended to replace the Boeing B-52 Stratofortress in the 1960s, the B-70 was professed obsolete long before it flew; the reason was the intercontinental ballistic missile.

The B-52 was not replaced by the B-70. Whether or not it is replaced by the Rockwell B-1, or the Northrop B-2 "stealth" bomber now under development, remains to be seen.

Since 1975, the USSR has been producing an intercontinental strategic bomber, the Tupoley Tu-26. The North Atlantic Treaty Organization has given the Tu-26 the code name of "Backfire." It is capable of reaching American soil at doublesonic speeds and is armed with a variety of free falling and stand-off air-to-surface weapons. Experts estimate that the USSR had at least 120 of these bombers in 1978, and that total Tu-26 Backfire production could reach 400 aircraft. Like the United States, Russia has an awesome force of ICBMs but continues to produce manned bombers.

Fifteen years of research and development and $1.5 billion were spent building and perfecting a bomber that the Air Force wanted and needed. However, politics and the progressing development of the ICBM changed the priorities.

The B-70 was initially for subsonic cruising and supersonic dashing but in the long process of testing it became a long range high altitude triplesonic experiment in flight. Of particular note was its structure for achieving high speeds. At a time when 40,000-pound fighter interceptor craft could barely attain doublesonic speeds, the one-half-million-pound XB-70A exceeded three times the speed of sound. The Valkyrie was designed to make use of a then little understood phenomenon called "compression lift." Compression lift occurs when the shock wave generated by the shape of an airplane flying at high supersonic speeds actually supports part of the airplane's weight. For additional lift and improved stability at both transonic and supersonic speeds, the B-70 could droop its wingtips from zero to sixty-five degrees. This feature effectively boxed in the flow of air underneath the B-70 so it could ride upon the compressed mass of air which it created.

The B-70 died in infancy, never having the opportunity of proving its worth; overtaken by the progress of which the plane itself had become a symbol. It provided the aerospace industry with a wealth of data for future programs. The B-70 was a watershed project; its legacy is well recalled by the last unique, futuristic B-70 bird standing erect on its landing gear in the Air Force Museum, poised as if waiting for one more takeoff.

TABLE OF CONTENTS

XB-70A-1 shown in USAF Plant 42 hangar at Palmdale the evening before roll-out.   Rockwell

Chapter One
Historical Overview

I. Introduction

High military officials often design and endorse weapons that might have won the previous war. Other men, rarer in mold, endowed with foresight, envision weapons that may be useful in future confrontations. One such man was Major General William (Billy) Mitchell. From the harassing "by hand" bombing sorties of World War One, Mitchell extrapolated vast aerial squadrons devastating all in their path. However, in pleading his case with military planners he was met with laughter and contempt.

During the period July 13–21, 1921, Mitchell's U.S. Army Air Corps Martin MB-2 bombers unloaded a bevy of bombs during a series of Army and Navy bombing tests sending captured German warships to Davy Jones' Locker off the Virginia coast.

Proudly, Mitchell pointed to the sinking hulks and said, "That's what a bomber can do!"

Unconvinced, the conservative American armed forces hierarchy derided Mitchell's theories and persisted in their reliance on conventional weapons, especially naval sea power. But Mitchell would not be put aside and, unfortunately, his constant criticism of the current trends led to his unjust court martial in 1925. He was stripped of his command and reduced from the rank of brigadier general to colonel. Billy Mitchell died at the age of 57 on February 19, 1936. He was posthumously reinstated to the rank of major general and is regarded today as one of the principal architects of American Air Power.

Foreign powers were not blind to occurrences across the ocean. Germany demonstrated that fact during the Spanish Civil War of 1936, employing bomber aircraft as an integrated element of their infamous blitzkrieg. This German head start led to early dominance of World War Two and prompted the United States to belatedly champion progressive bombers of its own.

First of 512 Boeing B-17E-BO Flying Fortress bombers during flight test over Puget Sound near Seattle, Washington. More than any other Allied bomber the B-17, flying continuous bombing runs over Germany, contributed to VE Day.   *Boeing*

Most produced Allied bomber during WWII was the Consolidated B-24 Liberator. Liberator in foregound is first B-24D-105-CO from batch of 45. Photo illustrates just what wartime mass-production was all about.
General Dynamics

The youthful American aircraft industry responded with the following bomber types: the Boeing B-17 Flying Fortress, Consolidated B-24 Liberator, North American B-25 Mitchell, Martin B-26 Marauder, Consolidated B-32 Dominator, and the atomic bomb-dropping B-29 Superfortress. These bombers significantly contributed to the Allied Victory. Mitchell's vision was realized.

With this fulfillment of Mitchell's vision, what was required was a new vision of the future; a vision of airpower in the nuclear age. General Curtis E. Lemay, a bomber pilot during WWII, became the next champion of American airpower. Appointed commander in chief of the USAF Strategic Air Command in 1948, it was his B-29s which, in a mere three months during the Korean War, systematically destroyed all the major industrial targets of North Korea. When, in August of 1953, the Soviet Union exploded its first hydrogen bomb, it was LeMay who expedited all phases of SAC training, who oversaw the swift introduction of the new jet bombers to replace the B-29s and

Named after General William "Billy" Mitchell, one of the principal architects of American Air Power, the North American B-25 Mitchell is credited with the first successful retaliation against Japan. On 18 April 1942, 16 B-25s, led by then Lt. Col. James H. "Jimmy" Doolittle, left the aircraft carrier Hornet and bombed Tokyo among other selected targets. It was the first time since Pearl Harbor that U.S. forces hit back at Japan.
Rockwell

B-50s and who began planning for nuclear deterrents.

Second B-26B-45-MA from a batch of 91. Martin built 5,157 B-26 Marauders for WWII action. After its wingspan had been increased from 65 feet to 71 feet it became one of the most respected bombers in WWII, pilots raved about its capabilities. *Martin Marietta*

Second B-32-1-CF of 10. Named Dominator, Consolidated's B-32 was produced as a long-range heavy bomber, and, if Boeing's B-29 had failed to become the great bomber it was, B-32s may have been called upon to drop atom bombs on Japan instead. 115 B-32s were built during WWII. *General Dynamics*

On 6 and 9 August 1945 two different Boeing B-29 Superfortress's (Enola Gay and Bock's Car) dropped atomic bombs on Hiroshima and Nagasaki, Japan, thus speeding up VJ Day and bringing an end to WWII. Third XB-29-BO is shown. *Boeing via Williams*

Boeing's B-50 heavy bomber served as an interim strategic bomber until B-47s gained squadron strength in the SAC organization. Shown is a B-50D-115-BN from a batch of 33. The B-50 is sometimes referred to as Superfortress 2, owing to its resemblance to B-29s. Note that both bomb bays are open. Boeing

In October 1954, LeMay put forth a mission requirement for a new, advanced jet bomber. He formally requested that the Department of Defense investigate the possiblity of developing an advanced jet-powered bomber for the 1965–1975 time period to replace B-52s and B-58s, which hadn't entered service yet. He wanted a bomber that had the range and payload-carrying capability of the B-52 and the speed of the B-58. His proposed bomber was to use existing runways and maintenance facilities. Further, it was to carry a 50,000 pound payload 6,000 nautical miles (nm) with "as high a speed as possible" over its target. The USAF Air Research and Development Command followed LeMay's lead and issued Weapon System Requirements WS-110A and

WS-125A, that requested an industry-wide study of an advanced bomber for SAC. Requirements called for the proposed bomber to have a Mach 0.9 cruise speed to an area some 1,000 nm from its target, then "dash" at its maximum possible speed (hopefully Mach 2-plus) to and from its target at high altitude, then slow again to Mach 0.9 cruise speed for its trip home. This split-mission requirement coined the phrase subsonic cruise—supersonic dash. As required, the WS-110A was to burn conventional jet fuel while the WS-125A was to be propelled by nuclear fuel. Capable of carrying 25-ton bomb loads, both bomber types were to carry a full complement of varied weapons either nuclear or conventional.

Another interim SAC bomber was Consolidated's B-36 "Peacemaker." This 10-engined monster served SAC well until the advent of Boeing's 8-jet B-52. Neither the B-36 nor B-50 fired a shot in anger. Shown is a B-36D. General Dynamics

III. Competition

It was during February of 1955 that the ARDC issued its WS-110A/WS-125A requirements to the industries. SAC hoped one or both of these advanced bomber proposals would be operational by 1963. By July 1955, the WS-110A bomber proposal included an intercontinental photo reconnaissance version designated WS-110L. Thus the program became known as WS-110A/L. On July 16, 1955, six airframe contractors—Convair, Lockheed, Martin, Douglas, Boeing and North American were awarded similar exploratory contracts to investigate WS-110A/L requirements. The challenge of creating a subsonic cruise—supersonic dash bomber capable of carrying 25-ton bomb loads over great distances was met with eager if somewhat misguided enthusiasm.

Convair and Lockheed were selected to pursue the WS-125A nuclear powered bomber. Martin and Douglas were busy developing intercontinental ballistic missiles (ICBM). Therefore, the competition to build the WS-110A/L narrowed to two companies, the Boeing Airplane Company and North American Aviation, Inc. On November 11, 1955, both companies were issued letters of intent for WS-110A/L

General Dynamic's B-58 Hustler was the first supersonic bomber in the world. First flown on 11 November 1956, the Hustler offered its advanced technologies, including honeycomb sandwich construction, to the development of the XB-70A. LeMay wanted a bomber with the speed of a B-58 and the range of a B-52, thus the B-70 was created.

General Dynamics

Boeing B-52B-BO Stratofortress assigned to March AFB, California, circa 1955. This particular "B" was designated RB-52B and served as a reconnaissance bomber as well as strategic bomber. This aircraft was delivered to SAC 29 June 1955.

Boeing

parallel studies. Then on December 9, 1955, each firm was granted an engineering study contract to complete their respective proposals, each to build a full-scale engineering WS-110A/L mockup including wind tunnel models. Pratt & Whitney, Rolls-Royce, Curtiss-Wright, and General Electric began their battle to develop a suitable powerplant.

On March 5, 1956, two NACA (now NASA) aerodynamicists, Clarence A. Syvertson and Alfred J. Eggers, published a top secret paper dealing with a phenomenon Eggers had discovered in 1954 while mowing his lawn called "Compression Lift." The paper is entitled, "*Aircraft Configurations Developing High Lift/ Drag Ratios at High Supersonic Speeds,*" NACA Publication RM-A55105. As it turned out they had correctly theorized that shock waves generated by an airplane during supersonic flight could be incorporated to produce additional lift. Neither Boeing nor North American knew of this aerodynamic find in 1956. But a search through scientific periodicals later by North American brought the concept to light.

Further development of the WS-110L photo-reconnaissance version was terminated on June 7, 1956, as Lockheed's U-2 was then under secret development and it was to play that role.

Both companies presented their initial WS-110A proposals for USAF/ARDC evaluation in October of 1956, following a one-year study. To meet range and supersonic dash speed requirements both designs were gargantuan and heavy. Boeing's Model 724, WS-110A carried a takeoff gross weight of 610,000 pounds while North American's Model NA-239, WS-110A entry tipped the scales at 750,000 lb. at takeoff. Each design featured "floating wingtips," a term coined by Boeing, that attached to the main wing until the bomber came within 1,000 nm of its target. At this time they would be jettisoned leaving the primary aircraft to continue on at supersonic speeds. These floating wingtips carried podded fuel tanks with their own flying surfaces, the fuel tanks were about the size of a B-47's fuselage and the entire wingtip/tank assembly weighed about 190,000 lb. fueled. These three-part aircraft were some 150 feet long, spanned about 260 feet, and stood approximately 40 ft. high. Boeing's design was to be powered by four GE X275 turbojet engines, North American opted for six. Both proposals featured foreplanes, canard-type control surfaces. But North American's arrowhead-like canard effectively obscured 50 percent of the pilot's forward vision. As split-mission bombers, they were to take off and cruise subsonically to an area some 1,000 nm from their target, jettison their wingtips, then dash supersonically to and from their target.

It was in January of 1957 that North American discovered NACA's Compression Lift paper written by Syvertson and Eggers, they immediately began to study it in detail.

It took only four months for the USAF/ARDC to evaluate the Boeing and North American WS-110A proposals. On March 11, 1957, both designs were returned postage due! LeMay was not happy. Upon seeing the artist's concepts he commanded, "Back to the drawing boards. These aren't airplanes—they're three-ship formations!" LeMay knew what he wanted and felt strongly that both firms could produce better aircraft.

The second WS-110A competition was fierce. Both companies scratched and clawed for technical breakthroughs. Tricks like NASA's Area Rule, variable-geometry flying surfaces, high-cycle engines, exotic fuels, advanced aerodynamics, and structures were investigated, applied where necessary. Both firms reconfigured. North American applied NACA's Compression Lift to its new design and both companies opted to use six engines that burned boron, a high-energy chemical "zip" fuel that increased both speed and range. Both designs therefore became known as "chemically-powered bombers," or CPBs. With six engines burning boron, Mach 3 cruise at 70,000 feet became possible, and unrefueled range increased to 7,600 nautical miles.

Boeing's new WS-110A CPB effort appeared as its Model 804, a 200-foot long delta-winged design with retractable canard foreplanes that resembled its Bomarc pilotless ground-to-air interceptor missile. Their rejuvenated studies of aircraft configurations, aerodynamics, metallurgy, and the use of boron fuel prescribed the use of six underwing, podded General Electric X279E turbo-ramjet engines. Maximum takeoff weight had dropped to an acceptable 499,500 pounds. The deficiencies of their previous design had been cured. Its revamped design now boasted of a rocket-like airframe and matchless performance. In fact, its GE engines were rated at Mach 4! It was well received.

To take full advantage of NACA's Compression Lift, North American also reconfigured. Its WS-110A CPB now featured large delta wings with variable geometry (v-g) tips to be folded downward during flight for increased stability and lift at high supersonic speeds. It retained a foreplane but this was relocated to an area behind the cockpit, reducing interference with the pilot's vision. It sported twin vertical stabilizers and its engines, six GE J93-GE-5 boron-burners, were located side-by-side in a huge

Initial WS-110/XB-70 proposal from North American, like Boeing's, featured jettisonable "floating wingtips," with huge external fuel tanks approximating the size of a B-47's fuselage. Rejected, these designs were to cruise subsonically to an area some 1,000 nm from target, then dash supersonically to and away from it. LeMay frowned on these designs and barked, "Back to the drawing boards. These aren't airplanes, they are three-ship formations."
Rockwell via Boswell

box-like structure underneath the fuselage and wing assemblies. A two-position v-g windscreen, down for low speed and up for high speed operations, was incorporated. Gross takeoff weight was estimated at 500,000 lb.

The time came to put all theories to the test. Both companies had fought hard to gain technical advantages in performance to meet stringent Air Force demands for such a highly sophisticated weapon system. The planes that had been a mishmash had metamorphosed into global travelers capable of sustained M3 cruise at 70,000 feet. And with the benefit of boron fuel, each bomber could now fly to and from their target without the aid of inflight refueling. Since both firms had failed to satisfy USAF/ARDC with their initial designs a Phase I, Part II competition for the WS-110A CPB was agreed to. This agreement, however, specified that their new proposals must include detailed descriptions of all major sub-systems within their respective designs.

Boeing, advised to investigate compression lift, did not. They were highly skeptical and didn't think North American's revised lift over drag figures were valid, or that their new design would reach the stated goal. Thus Boeing stood pat with its WS-110A offering.

In July 1957, LeMay's vision was passed on to General Thomas S. Power, who had been LeMay's Vice Commander at SAC from 1948 to 1954. Since that time Power had headed the ARDC; he now became SAC's new Commander in Chief. Power had great knowledge of bomber aircraft, including the WS-110A CPB, and was well informed about oncoming intercontinental ballistic missiles. His job was to create a mixed bomber and missile force for SAC.

Boeing and North American resubmitted their respective designs in August 1957. As the date of the Air Force decision neared, the atmosphere surrounding the competitors became charged with high tension. Rumors, unsubstantiated and vague, were rife. Executives hovered like birds of prey.

During September of 1957 the Air Force evaluated Boeing's second WS-110 proposal at its Seattle, Washington, Plant 2 facility. In October 1957, the Air Force did the same at North American's Los Angeles, California facility. Both firms had much, much better offerings this time.

Then on December 23, 1957, the decision came down. North American got the nod. They would build the WS-110A CPB. Boeing, shock-

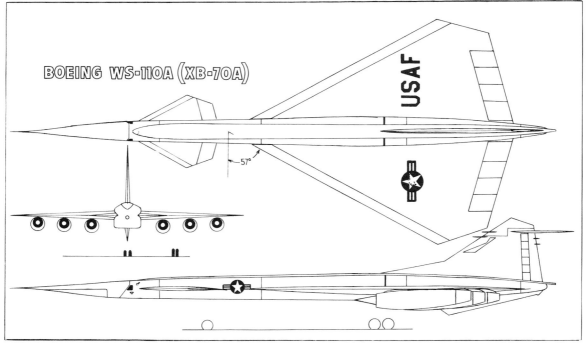

Artist's impression of Boeing's XB-70 proposal.
Author's Collection

BOEING WS-110A (XB-70A)

←57°

USAF

Illustration shows general layout of Boeing's XB-70 proposal which appeared close in resemblance to that firm's Bomarc ground-to-air pilotless interceptor. Not drawn to scale.
Author's Collection.

Artist's concept illustrating how North American's redesigned XB-70 was to appear. Actual aircraft looked just like this drawing. Shown is M3 cruise configuration, the wingtips are full-down.

Rockwell

ed over the decision, demanded and got a congressional inquiry which later determined that NAA's superior lift over drag figures had convinced the Air Force and KO'd Boeing's challenger.

On January 2, 1958, NAA was contracted (AF-36599) to construct a full-scale engineering mockup of its then Model NA-259, WS-110A under Phase I. In addition, NAA was made the prime contractor for the entire WS-110A program except for the engines which became the sole responsibility of the General Electric Company. It was at this time that GE was contracted to build its YJ93-GE-5 boron-burner. Shortly after USAF go-ahead NAA's other rival bomber, Convair's WS-125A Nuclear Powered Bomber, was cancelled. The WS-110A would be SAC's only new bomber. The Air Force announced an 18-month acceleration in the WS-110 program and moved the first flight up from December 1963 to December 1961. SAC was to receive its first WS-110A in December 1963, its first combat ready wing of 12 aircraft in August 1964.

On February 6, 1958, the WS-110A designation was abolished in favor of a more traditional B-for-bomber classification: XB-70.

During April 1958, a Weapon System Evaluation Conference between North American and the Air Research and Development Command was held, after which, several XB-70 design changes were made, including an increase in its design gross weight to facilitate greater payloads.

In May 1958, NAA began sub-contracting. The IBM Corporation was to produce the B-70's stellar-inertial bombing-navigation system; AiResearch its air data computing sys-

Publicity photo depicting a Valkyrie with an XB-70A.

Rockwell

tem; Westinghouse its electronic countermeasures (ECM) defense system; Boeing its wings; GE its "unjammable" radar; Lockheed its aft fuselage section; Chance Vought its tail assemblies and elevons; Cleveland Pneumatic its landing gear; Sundstrand its secondary power systems; Sperry its twin-gyro stellar platform; Autonetics its navigation system (not to be confused with IBM's bombing-navigation system); Oster its engine instrumentation system; and Beech its still top secret "alert pod"

15

that was to go with the B-70 everywhere for a quick getaway. This so-called "alert pod" could only be called "a special power device" by its manufacturer, Beech. Ultimately, some 2,000 sub-contractors become involved in the B-70 program.

SAC wanted their new bomber to have an official name and held a service-wide contest to name the plane. Out of 20,000 entries submitted, the winner was Valkyrie, the beautiful maidens of Norse myth who roamed the skies on their steeds deciding the fate of battle casualties. The name Valkyrie became official 3 July 1958.

By mid-summer '58, GE had successfully bench run and flight tested its YJ93-GE-5 boron-burner. General Electric used Convair's third B-58A, 55-0662, for its inflight engine test bed. Redesignated NB-58A, it was equipped with a special engine nacelle housing a J93 that was suspended underneath the B-58's fuselage on centerline where its component (weapon/fuel) pod was normally carried. During these flight tests speeds of Mach 2-plus were attained.

On December 31, 1958, NAA was contracted (AF-38669) to build a single Model NA-264, XB-70 under Phase II, Part I, as a follow-on program to its Model NA-259, XB-70.

During March 1959, Air Force engineers

During formal XB-70A mockup inspection, models were displayed. One set of models compared XB-70 to a B-52. Another model of an XB-70 thrilled would-be pilots. Shown left to right are Joe Cotton, Fitz Fulton, and Al White. Gentleman between Fulton and White isn't known by this writer. *Rockwell via Boswell*

16

Boeing KC-135A Stratotanker tops off B-52G fuel tanks inflight. Although JP-6 burning J93 cut XB-70's range by 10 per cent, an inflight drink from KC-135 satisfied its mission range requirements. Shown are 4th B-52G and 219th KC-135A.
Boeing via Brooks

(more than 200) inspected NAA's XB-70 mock-up at the first Development Engineering Inspection. Over a ten day period, every detail of the bomber as both a weapons system and as an airplane was examined minutely. In April NAA held its first formal mockup conference. Twenty technical teams went over the B-70's operational capabilities. Colonel John J. Smith, ARDC Deputy Chief of Strategic Systems, chaired the mockup conference while Col. Ted L. Bishop, who had chaired the DEI, served as the mockup conference recorder. After the B-70 mockup conference, 761 changes were requested in its design.

On July 27, 1959, under the previous contract, a Phase II, Part II redirection came down as a follow-on program to the Model NA-264, B-70. After this, the B-70 became known as Model NA-267.

On August 10, 1959, the expensive boron chemical fuel program was cancelled. This in turn axed GE's YJ93-GE-5 boron-burner. However, GE had another version of its J93 that burned JP-6, a highly refined jet petroleum fuel, called the YJ93-GE-3. Without boron, the B-70's range was sliced by 10%. But a single inflight refueling by a KC-135 Stratotanker satisfied mission requirements, gave the B-70 its 7,000-plus nm range.

On September 23, 1959, NAA's Model NA-257, F-108 (previously WS-202A) Rapier, a Mach 3 long range interceptor being developed in parallel, was cancelled. This immediately increased B-70 program costs by $150 million, as development costs of it and the B-70 were shared.

The F-108 was nearly identical to the B-70 structurally and was to employ most of its same sub-systems. It was to be powered by two

J93-GE-3s instead of the six required by its cousin. It would have been operated by a crew of two; pilot and fire control officer. The Rapier's advanced Hughes-built AN/ASG-18 radar and fire control system and AIM-47 Falcon nuclear-tipped air-to-air intercept missile continued in development, and were used later in Lockheed's exotic M3.5 YF-12A interceptor prototypes. The F-108's projected performance equalled that of the B-70: speed, range, and altitude. It was to be a large interceptor weighing 102,000 pounds at its design gross weight, 73,000 lb. at combat weight, and 48,000 lb. empty and it was to be 85 feet long, 22 ft. high, and span 53 ft.; wing area was 1,400 square feet. The F-108 was scheduled to fly in March 1961. When it was cancelled it had only progressed to mockup stage.

IV. Politics

On December 3, 1959, the American air arm, reaching into the 1960s, was severed at the wrist. Task force studies indicated that a long term reassessment of the manned bomber program, especially its weapon systems, was in order. Maurice Stans, budget director for the Eisenhower Administration, who extolled the virtues of ICBMs, was searching frantically for a way of balancing the budget during Eisenhower's last year in office. He seized upon the task force study and brandished it. The B-70 program was cancelled. Only the single B-70 prototype under construction, GE's work on its YJ93-GE-3 engines, and IBM's investigatory work on its ASQ-28 bombing-navigation system continued but, all at a reduced rate. All other sub-contracts were cancelled. The lone B-70 was rescheduled to fly in December of 1962 (a one-year setback), with continued

Proposed M3 long-range all-weather all-missile armed F-108 Rapier interceptor. Air Force cancelled F-108 on 23 September 1959, but its advanced Hughes-built AN/ASG-18 radar and fire control system and AIM-47 Falcon nuclear-tipped air-to-air missile continued in development, were used later in Lockheed's exotic M3.5 YF-12A interceptor prototypes.
Rockwell

flight testing until 1967. But the Air Force had not given up; they wanted their 2,000 mph bombers and they wanted them in squadrons.

It was during the late '50s and early '60s that ICBMs had emerged as a reliable weapon system that cost a fraction of their manned counterparts. Their lower cost, coupled with the fact that human life (aircraft crewmembers) would be spared, strongly enticed military planners, and, the missile-versus-bomber debates were born.

Pro-missile advocates argued that their lower cost, pinpoint accuracy, intercontinental range and rapid reaction time made ICBMs superior to manned bombers. Pro-bomber advocates countered with the fact that manned bombers can be recalled; they submitted that once an ICBM is launched it is committed to strike its programmed target and that it cannot change its mind. Moreover, they argued that since an ICBM requires a mere 30 minutes or so to reach its target, there wouldn't be enough time for negotiations, that an all-out nuclear confrontation could ensue. These arguments grew heated and persist today.

However, persuasive arguments, particularly those of USAF Chief of Staff Thomas White and USAF Deputy Chief of Development Roscoe C. Wilson, led to the reallotment of monies by Congress to the B-70 program in mid-1960. General Wilson, who hoped for possible "squadron strength" by 1966 said, "While we need the brute power of ICBMs, they lack the flexibility essential to winning a military victory. We will continue to need manned aircraft to seek out hidden and mobile targets, to restrike residual targets and perform a variety of other tasks. We look forward to the B-70, which is now under development, as the essential partner of the ICBMs."

On July 31, 1960, Congress approved an additional $75 million, increasing total appropriations for fiscal year 1961 to $365 million. This amount made it possible to complete the B-70 prototype, provide a structural loads static test airframe, reinstate all sub-contractor work, and build 12 fully operational B-70s.

On September 21, 1960, NAA was contracted (AF-42058) to build a single Model NA-274, YB-70 as a follow-on to its Model NA-267, XB-70. It was to be completed with the installation of the full weapon system and have provisions for an operational four-man crew; AF (AF-42058) to build two Model NA-278, XB-70s

Lockheed's YF-12A "Blackbird" may have been responsible for the demise of both the North American F-108 Rapier and B-70. It had undergone secret flight testing to speeds near M3.5 at altitudes above 70,000 feet long before XB-70A-1 flew.   Lockheed via Ferguson

in addition to the single YB-70; AF issued serial numbers 62-0001 and 62-0207. Overall B-70 cost to date was $1.3 billion.

Soon after John F. Kennedy took office as President of the United States, a controversial announcement emanated from the White House. Following recommendation of his Defense Secretary Robert S. McNamara, President Kennedy effectively sounded the death knell of the B-70 as an operational bomber.

Kennedy released an official statement in March 1961, which said in part that America's forthcoming missile capabilities "makes unnecessary and economically unjustifiable the development of the B-70 as a full weapons system at this time."

The president further recommended that the B-70 program "be carried forward, essentially to explore the problems of flying at three times the speed of sound with an airframe potentially useful as a bomber, through the development of a small number of prototype aircraft and related bombing and navigation systems."

Thus in April 1961, McNamara cut NAA's authorization to three aircraft, which were to be built as aerodynamic high speed research aircraft. On April 10, NAA was contracted (AF-42058) to build two Model NA-278, XB-70 prototypes in addition to the single YB-70 AF issued serial numbers 62-0001 and 62-0207. Overall B-70 cost to date was $1.3 billion.

On July 31, 1961, the $365 million amount already voted was trimmed to $75 million, and, the B-70's first flight date, already set back, was set back again, this time to December of 1963. The meager $75 million budget now covered only a single XB-70 prototype stripped of its complex weapon systems. These were to be incorporated later in the YB-70 and production B-70s following installation and evaluation within the XB-70.

In January 1962, McNamara defined the

Boeing B-52G Stratofortress with two North American AGM-28 Hound Dog missiles, and B-52H with four Douglas GAM-87 Skybolt missiles. Both missile types were considered to be B-70 armament as well.
Boeing via Brooks

XB-70A-1 being towed out of its final assembly building for official roll-out ceremonies May 11, 1964. About 5,000 spectators witnessed the historic occasion. Building across the way with North American Aviation, Inc. on it is where XB-70A-2 rolled-out from May 29, 1965. Rockwell via Boswell

government's position when he said, "Considering the increasing capabilities of surface-to-air interceptor missiles, the speed and altitude of the B-70 would no longer be a very significant advantage. Furthermore, it has been designed without the adaptive capabilities of using air-to-surface missiles such as Hound Dog and Skybolt, and in a low-altitude attack it must fly at subsonic speeds. In addition, the B-70 is not well suited to an era in which both sides have large numbers of ICBMs. It would be more vulnerable on the ground than hardened missiles, and it does not lend itself to airborne alert measures."

Hopes were raised repeatedly by B-70 proponents, but each attempt was promptly squelched by McNamara. A last ditch effort to resuscitate the bomber was made by the Air Force when it changed its classification to reconnaissance-strike, creating the RS-70. Hoping against hope, the USAF proposed a program of 60 operational RS-70s by 1969, at an estimated cost of $50 million each, with another 150 to be delivered in 1970.

In July, 1963, the House Armed Services Committee, headed by Carl Vinson, requested $491 million for three RS-70 prototypes. Congress, however, only allocated an additional $52.9 million thereby reaching a total of $275.9 million, far short of the required amount. As no further funds were forthcoming, the RS classification was dropped.

By August 1963, GE's YJ93-GE-3 had com-

XB-70A-1 after roll-out on May 11, 1964. Note large rectangular air inlet throats; an average height man could stand up within these and walk to its engines. Rockwell via Boswell

pleted 3,500 hours of bench testing up to 70,000-foot altitudes. Five hundred fifty hours were completed at Mach 2 and, 33,000 pounds static sea level thrust in afterburner had been attained (3% less than the YJ-93-5 boron-burner version).

21

XB-70A-1 with X-15A-2 at Edwards Air Force Base.   NASA

On March 5, 1964, the B-70 program was reduced to two XB-70(A) prototypes. This eliminated the YB-70 variant which was well along in fabrication. It was scrapped. It was now apparent that the lone function of the B-70 was to be a guinea pig for the American SST. It had become a sheep in wolf's clothing.

On May 11, 1964, the official XB-70 rollout ceremony was held at North American's Los Angeles Division, Air Force Plant 42, Palmdale, California; Eighteen months late, but a sight to see. Valkyrie, white and gleaming under the bright California sun, was set free at last from the confines of her hangar.

The crowd of well wishers present for the ceremony found her spellbinding. The huge delta wings, the serpentine-like fuselage supporting canards, and twin vertical tails set her apart from any airplane seen before. On the ground, it appeared to be traveling 2,000 mph. Yet what had started as a first line SAC bomber some ten years earlier was already being proclaimed obsolete. And it hadn't even flown.

V. Summary

It is unfortunate that politics and ICBMs played such major roles in the demise of the B-70. But more than anything, or anyone, it was Robert McNamara who contributed to the death of the B-70. In fact, he actually refused to release monies already procured for the B-70 by congress. But in all fairness to Mr. McNamara there may have been another important factor. While North American developed its B-70 outwardly, Lockheed designed, built, and flight tested its A-12 (which evolved into the YF-12, then SR-71) in total secrecy. Records now show that Lockheed began flight testing its advanced manned interceptor (AMI), A-11-CUM-YF-12A on April 26, 1962—that is, two years before the B-70's rollout. And, the YF-12A's existence wasn't announced until July 24, 1964, when President Johnson said, "The performance of the YF-12A far exceeds that of any other aircraft in the world today. It has already demonstrated speeds in excess of Mach 3 at altitudes above 70,000 feet." This, of course, put the B-70 program at a disadvantage as XB-70 No. 1 wasn't to fly for two months.

Whether or not the B-70 program was cancelled because of any of these foregoing reasons remains unclear, but each factor did contribute.

Chapter Two
Developmental Highlights

The creation of such an advanced airplane was not an easy task. There is a formula in aircraft manufacturing which states that designers can only increase speed at the expense of range, or vice versa. Yet, to get past the drawing boards, the B-70 had to violate this conservation formula.

As one expert noted, "A fighter is designed for speed; a bomber for range; a tanker for capacity. Combine these qualities and you get the B-70."

The B-70 accomplishment was primariy the result of clever aerodynamic design. Digging in the cluttered attic of flight history, North American engineers found a design feature which had not been used since Wilbur and Orville employed it. Dusted off and spruced up, this canard, or foreplane, was used to counteract trim changes occurring between stall speed (150 kias) and Mach 3 cruise. This negated the need for a conventional tailplane.

An additional task for the canard was to lower B-70's landing speeds to approximate those of conventional subsonic jet airliners, about 150 knots indicated airspeed. This was done by having the canard, which is placed behind the cockpit three-quarters of the way up the long, slender fuselage, equipped with flaps. Lowered 25 degrees these flaps were used in conjunction with the down-elevon to raise the nose of the B-70. Landings took place in this maximum lift configuration.

The most obvious visual characteristic of the Valkyrie was its large (6,297.15 square feet) area delta-shaped cantilevered wing. A less obvious feature was the v-g, folding wingtips which were used only during flight. As speed increased, the v-g tips were lowered to a maximum 65 degrees anhedral. Shock waves, generated by the tips, worked on the underside of the wings and increased lift. Also, this configuration improved directional stability and

XB-70A-1 being towed out for another flight test. Note large intake maws separated by wedge-shaped splitter plate, 17 x 8-foot radome and canards.
Rockwell

Wingtips mid-down, XB-70A-1 streaks across the skies over California's Mojave Desert. Note generated vortex coming off the top of fuselage.   *Rockwell via Boswell*

allowed the twin vertical fins and rudder assemblies to be reduced in size. Altogether, the v-g wingtips were responsible for a 5% increase in overall lift.

The B-70 was designed with twelve, trailing-edge elevons, six on each side of the engine bay. They were operated by 24 hydraulic actuators, independently worked via two hydraulic systems. To achieve longitudinal and lateral control, the elevons could deflect as much as 30 degrees up or down. When the wingtips were down the two outside elevons on each side locked.

To avoid high-drag shock waves at supersonic speeds, the B-70 as built with a v-g windscreen that retracted during subsonic flight for forward vision, or extended to streamline the nose during supersonic modes. In fact, the whole forward windshield was hinged and could be changed to the best aerodynamic slope.

An intake splitter duct, or wedge, on the underside of the wings and fuselage acted to create the phenomenon known as compression lift. By slowing the free flow M3 air stream to M2.3, it made a static pressure area in front of the shock wave. As the air flow above the wings continued at M3, the plane was boosted up.

It was the above feature that ended Boeing's bid to build the B-70. The NASA's Compression Lift theory was verified at North American through extensive wind tunnel test programs covering more than ten thousand hours. That testing started with simple, small exploratory models that were used to develop and confirm the compression lift theory. NAA's initial research and development program was followed by an intense investigation utilizing precision-made stainless steel models representing the actual airplane configuration (speeds up to M3.5 were investigated) cover-

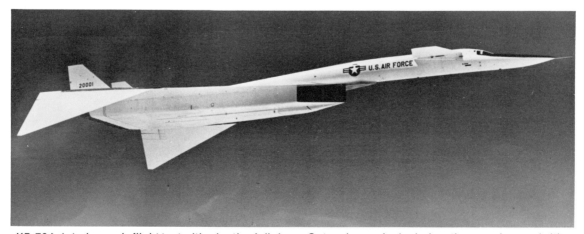

XB-70A-1 during early flight test with wingtips full-down. Outer elevons locked when tips were lowered either to mid-down or full-down deflection. When wingtips were full-down, another 5% lift was generated because wingtips boxed-in shock wave generated by them, adding to its compression lift profile. Wingtips operated via six Curtiss-Wright 32,000 to 1 hinge motors.   *Rockwell via Bear*

XB-70A-2 undergoing construction at USAF Plant 42 at Palmdale. Note elevon details and 5 degree wing dihedral, size of delta-wing in comparison to workmen. *Rockwell*

ing all phases of design-drag, inlet performance, stability and control. The craft's lift over drag ratio was plotted against its angle of attack, NAA found a 100-plus per cent gain at small AOA and a peak L/D 22% higher still at lower AOA. It was a find nothing short of fantastic. It was the stability and control tests that led NAA aerodynamicists to develop the B-70's v-g wingtips that could be folded down during flight from zero to 65 degrees.

One of the critical parameters in the determination of an airframe's cruise efficiency is the lift-to-drag relationship. Higher L/D ratios result in increased range. To attain the range required for NAA's B-70, it was necessary to obtain higher L/D ratios than conventional designs offered. In fact, the L/D requirement was

twice that shown for conventional configurations at high supersonic speeds.

Compression lift analyses, utilizing lift created by fuselage shock waves, theorized that a conventional supersonic fuselage is essentially symmetrical, enlarging from the nose section to a relatively constant diameter causing the compression, or lift, on the nose of the body at supersonic speeds to occur uniformly around the circumference. This resulting in zero net lift at zero angle of attack, thereby creating a certain amount of pressure drag behind the shock waves produced by the nose of the aircraft.

North American's engineers realized if the wing/fuselage were arranged in such a manner as to take advantage of the compression

Illustration shows subsonic and supersonic modes of B-70's variable-geometry two-position windshield. Pilots sat 110 feet ahead of the landing gear and about 30 feet up. Fulton said that there was some noise inside the B-70 when windshield was raised or lowered, that with the windshield ramp down, there were some conditions where turbulent air flow around windshield caused cockpit noise. Noise stopped when windshield was raised a few degrees.

two-position vg
windshield

supersonic

subsonic

Stainless steel wind tunnel models of XB-70 undergoing tests to speeds of M3.5. Testing validated NASA's Compression Lift theory where 30% of B-70's weight was effectively eliminated in flight. Note wingtips down in bottom view of B-70.

Rockwell via Boswell

General Electric technician checking over a YJ93-GE-3 engine before delivery. Six of these 30,000 lb. thrust engines were used to propel each XB-70A. Udimet 700, a nickel-base alloy, was used in the fabrication of its turbine blades. Engine thrust to weight ratio was above 5 to 1. Length of the J93 was 237 inches or 19¾ feet; diameter at face was 52.5 inches or 4.375 feet.   *General Electric*

by making it produce lift, the L/D ratio would be increased. Such a design meant a body continually enlarging with distance aft of the nose. NAA found that by using only the bottom half of the body, placing it under the wing, so that the leading-edge of the wing coincided with the body shock wave, design Mach number increased. This resulted in the under-surface of

the body and the under-surface of the wing having a compression or lifting force acting on it. It was also determined that the trailing-edge of the wing should be swept forward before it joined the body at its base.

To utilize the foregoing conclusions but apply them to a practical airplane configuration, several compromises were necessary. The use

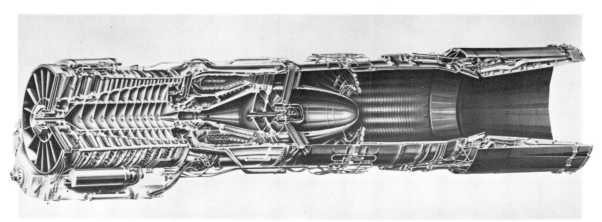

Cutaway detail of General Electric YJ93-GE-3 turbojet engine. Six of these engines powered XB-70A-2 to Mach 3.08 on 12 April 1966. J93 was basically an enlargement of GE's J79 which ultimately led to the development of GE's awesome 50,000 pound thrust GE 4 which had been slated for use on Boeing's proposed SST.   *General Electric*

of a forebody ahead of the wing, with canard suface, pilot enclosure and equipment, and the practical aspects of getting an efficient air inlet duct configuration with a practical engine arrangment, dictated a departure from the semi-cone, where its apex is at the leading-edge of the wing, approach. The XB-70 fuselage afterbody is located under the wing, and from a bottom view, forms a wedge originating at the wing leading-edge. The shock wave generated by the wedge corresponded to the wing leading-edge at the design mach number, which became M3-plus.

In effect then the wing had positive lift at zero AOA. The body volume and base areas were sized to the minimum to accommodate the required engines, fuel tanks, and related equipment. Thus no particular drag penalty was incurred. With the lift (net difference between pressures acting on upper and lower airfoil surfaces) obtained at zero AOA, the lift required for cruise flight at M3 was obtained at a lower AOA. Since drag-due-to-lift is proportional to the AOA, the result was lower drag-due-to-lift, and a higher L/D ratio was achieved. In fact, 30% of the B-70's weight was offset using compression lift.

In simpler terms, compression lift is achieved when the nose of the aircraft rams forward at supersonic speeds pushing air aside causing the air to wall up much like the bow wave made by a ship at sea. The wave is forced below the aircraft rather than above it due to the wedge shape of its design. Like a surfer then, the B-70 climbed on top of its shock waves and rode them out.

Mounted side-by-side, in the lower aft section of a 35-foot wide fuselage bay, were six GE YJ-93-GE-3 afterburning turbojet engines. Two v-g air intake inlets ahead of tunnels six feet high, 80 feet long, clinging to the underside of the B-70, fed the engines air.

To build the aircraft, North American developed new materials and ways to process them in order to meet the challenge of USAF requirements. Advanced methods of fabrication and construction were invented or improved upon before these exotic aircraft could be built. B-70 construction demanded new levels of precision welding, machining and sealing. Conceived in terms of 1950's technology, the Valkyrie itself was responsible for the advancement of precision manufacturing well into the 1960s.

With the B-70, advanced metallurgy came of age. Prolonged flight at M3 dictated that the Valkyrie be constructed of metal alloys able to withstand extreme temperatures. Some of these metals, such as stainless steel, titanium, nickel-base, and cobalt super alloys, were so new that the aerospace industry, North American in particular, was at a loss as to how to process them.

Aluminum's melting point is 1220° F compared to 2927° F for titanium; therefore titanium was the logical choice as temperatures were expected to reach up to 1000° F (enough to soften aluminum) in some areas. The amount of titanium used in the manufacture of each B-70 created 9.5% of their total structural weights. NAA's use of titanium alloys followed years of developmental work going beyond known titanium procedures to solve the technical problems associated with alloying, forming and fabricating.

Three different titanium alloys, all of which were heat-treated to high tensile strengths, were used in the construction of each B-70. One type was heat-treated to 160,000 pounds per square inch ultimate tensile strength in gauges of .030 to .070 thousandths of an inch. That particular titanium alloy was used to construct the forward 60-foot section of the aircraft where they were subjected to heat levels ranging from 450 to 500° F. The second and third types of titanium were heat-treated to 170,000 lb/psi and were used for internal and other structures.

Titanium alloys represented about 12,000 lb. of weight for each B-70; about 25% was plate 0.75 to 1.0 inch thick and another 25% was of heat-treated forgings and extrusions. For example, the B-70's windshield frame, which weighed some 200 lb. and measured 78 inches wide, was a heat-treated forging. The titanium used in the forward 60 feet of the B-70 aircraft consisted of about 12,000 individual details or parts.

B-70's canard foreplane and vertical tails were constructed with titanium substructures and stainless steel cover plates. Canard substructures were made of titanium alloy corrugated panels, sine wave welded. These panels reached temperatures of 400° F, while the steel skin covers reached 550° F. The twin vertical tails reached temperatures of 450 to 630° F where titanium was used, and higher still where steel was used. Structural loading throughout B-70 aircraft was extremely variable; however, certain titanium structures were designed for levels of stress reaching as high as 110,000 psi at room temperature, and to 0.67% of ksi at temperatures ranging from 450 to 550° F. B-70 airframes had a total dry weight of 128,000 lb.

Design speed of the B-70 was M3 (2,000 mph), but according to North American, its airframe design and materials used could have extended that maximum to M4, although major revisions of its environmental and hydraulic control systems would have been required. XB-70A-2 did reach M3.08. To accomplish that, the B-70 was a big user of brazed stainless steel honeycomb sandwich panels.

North American's B-70 program refined the use of stainless steel honeycomb sandwich panels. Furthermore, in recognition of NAA's leadership in developing titanium earlier as a useful aircraft metal alloy and for other achievements in the field of metallurgy, the American Society of Metals awarded its 1959 medal for the "Advancement of Research" to the then President of NAA, Inc., J. L. Atwood.

On each B-70, 68% or about 20,000 sq. ft. of stainless steel was used. The following are some representative aircraft component weight comparisons of the stainless steel honeycomb sandwich fabrication used throughout the B-70: wing, 10,965 lb.; fuselage, 9,640 lb.; canard box beam, 435 lb.; and vertical tail section, 955 lb. Had truss core sandwich been used instead, the additional 8,000 lb. weight per aircraft would have been prohibitive.

Brazed stainless steel honeycomb sandwich panel construction of B-70s were probably one of their most controversial features. NAA's answer to industry critics, who preferred the exclusive use of titanium alloys, was that brazed stainless steel honeycomb sandwich panels were light, strong, and had excellent insulation qualities.

The chief problem associated with brazed stainless steel honeycomb sandwich panels was skin detachment during high speed flight. XB70A-1 suffered from this dilemma several times, the worst when it lost a triangular section of its wing apex forward of its splitter plate and air inlets, causing severe engine damage. It later lost a 40x36 in. piece from the underside of its left wing, and an 8x38 in. strip from its right fuselage section later still. Loss of these skin panels occurred when thermal expansion and aerodynamic buffeting ballooned, or swelled, a defective area where the face sheet had cracked. This in turn led to the ripping away of the skin cover from the core in the voided area. Voids were started by air friction heating at high supersonic speeds. That heat build up weakened the metallic bond between the panel's face sheet where the brazings were too thin or poorly formed, aerodynamic pressure at high Mach aggravated the voids.

NAA engineers traced the immediate problem to construction processes. Improved fabrication techniques coupled with rigid quality control measures in the construction of XB-70A-2 reduced the problem greatly. However, one large piece did separate from the upper surface of its right wing during one high speed flight.

When a void was detected, it was usually repaired by welding pins between the outer and inner face sheets, through the honeycomb

XB-70A-2 roll-out May 29, 1965   Rockwell

structure. Another fix was a heat resistant sil-
icon putty called "red thunder" which was used
to fair smooth surfaces on each B-70. Pieces of
skin still came off during flight, but not as often.
If B-70 production had proceeded, a more permanent cure would have been necessary, of
course.

To design, engineer and build aircraft such
as the B-70 its program team members had to
solve extraordinary problems. Demanding
specifications motivated NAA's engineering
staff to investigate, reinvestigate every known
and unknown angle. For example, NAA engineers developed unique machines, one that
could "grind" metal, using a spark discharging
method that reversed the electroplating process; each spark that bounced off the metal
surface carried with it a microscopic speck of
metal. Another machine could take a metal
sheet 16 ft. wide and turn over a lip as minute
as 0.012 thousandths of an inch. Chemical
milling, a process usually reserved for pre-
liminary bulk reduction, evolved into an advanced method that produced aircraft parts only a
few thousandths of an inch thick from sheet
stock only 0.02 hundredths of an inch thick.

Advanced types of miniaturized and mech-
anized welding styles were developed for,
used successfully on both B-70 aircraft. Limit-
ed access to certain internal areas within the
B-70s during assembly led to the discovery of
the electron beam gun. This gun aimed a beam
of electrons to produce metal fusion in a narrow bead without resorting to weld filler materials. This welding method, called "LANAR" (low
amperage no added rod), allowed a weld bead
one-half normal thickness to be laid down on
each sheet face. These sheets were then roll
planished for smoothness and strength.

Sophisticated production methods alleviat-
ed most of the B-70's growing pains. However,
NAA's desire to create an advanced tri-sonic
SAC bomber was met by gremlins that refused
to play fair; the order of the day was, "Let's not
create a monster. Let's master one."

XB-70A-2 roll-out May 29, 1965.   Rockwell

One such gremlin was fuel tank sealing. This
originally became a monstrous problem NAA
had to master if its plane was to be successful.
XB-70A-1 was scheduled to fly in December
1963 but that date was bypassed as production problems, especially fuel tank sealing,
continued unsolved. Its JP-6 fuel was to be
encased with nitrogen to prevent auto-ignition
at high temperatures. It was imperative for fuel
tanks to be gas-tight. Yet the welding seals
near the hydraulic and electrical tubes and
wires, which pierced through fuel tank walls,
resisted sealants. The nitrogen gas escaped.

After months of failures, an organic rubber-
like substance called Viton B was painted on
leak areas. Between six and ten coats were

applied, each cured for six hours using electric heat of 350° F. This cure, after some 18 months of exploratory fixes, did the trick.

Throughout aviation history no airframe contractor had ever attempted such a challenging project as that of building the B-70s, the Air Force was very much aware of this fact. So although construction of the B-70 got behind chronologically, it was so far ahead technologically, that the Air Force was accordingly patient. Most problems plaguing XB-70A-1 were cured and their solutions were passed on to XB-70A-2, which, in turn, rolled out on May 29, 1965.

XB-70A-1 during flight No. 1 at 16.000 feet accompanied by two Northrop T-38A Talon chase planes. Note that engine area isn't painted white; this area was painted white later. Evidently a paint was found that didn't burn off due to engine heat.

Rockwell

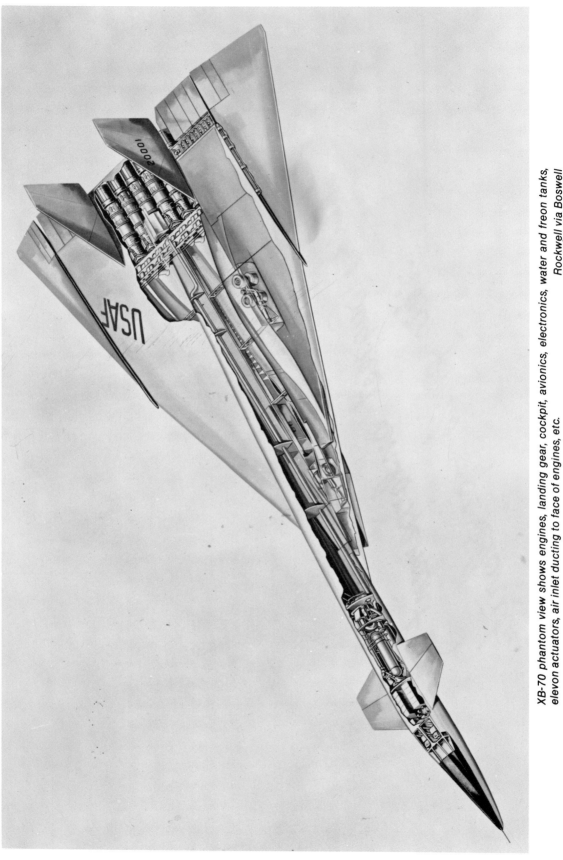

XB-70 phantom view shows engines, landing gear, cockpit, avionics, electronics, water and freon tanks, elevon actuators, air inlet ducting to face of engines, etc.
Rockwell via Boswell

Chapter Three
Configuration

The following excerpts deal with the structural design of the B-70 and is presented here with the permission of Richard L. Schleicher, Sc. D., from his presentation to the Institute of Aeronautical Sciences in 1967. At that time, Dr. Schleicher was Special Assistant to the Chief Engineer, North American Aviation, Inc. In 1971, after 42 years in aircraft structure engineering, Dr. Schleicher retired from North American Aviation, Inc. (now Rockwell International, North American Aircraft Operations).

The structural design of the XB-70 represents an integrated and highly coordinated program of advanced structures technology, materials and processes development, and the establishing of new manufacturing and inspection techniques. As a supersonic intercontinental bomber, it required designing the structure for a Mach 3.0 environment. The cruise requirements raised the structural temperatures beyond the capability of the aluminum alloys and, consequently, steel came into prominence as a structural material, although not to be used exclusively. Titanium and other materials also played significant roles. The physi-

cal arrangement of the aircraft was unique, and this required a high degree of technical skill and ingenuity in formulating the structural configuration. The thermal protection, without added insulation, of the large quantity of fuel carried, placed an additional function on the primary structure. Structural stiffness and aerodynamic smoothness had greater influence than experienced on other contemporary supersonic air vehicles. Finally, the manufacturing problems that arose exceeded the most difficult ever encountered. Nevertheless, the two aircraft that remained to be built from the original program were successfully completed and have demonstrated that sustained Mach 3 cruise is now an established fact.

The XB-70A's overall dimensions are roughly comparable to contemporary large aircraft with a length of 185 feet, a span of 105 feet, and a height of 30 feet. The weight of the vehicle exceeds one-half million pounds and most of this is fuel. The aircraft is characterized by a large delta wing with folding tips, a long slender forward fuselage supporting a canard, an intermediate body located beneath the wing, and an afterbody

XB-70A-2 in foreground, XB-70A-1 in background. Note A/V-2's 5 degree wing dihedral, amount of ground support equipment. This is one of the few photographs taken with both Valkyrie aircraft shown together.
Rockwell

33

XB-70 AIRFRAME

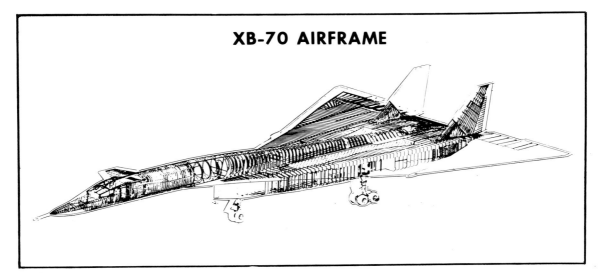

AIR VEHICLE TEMPERATURES

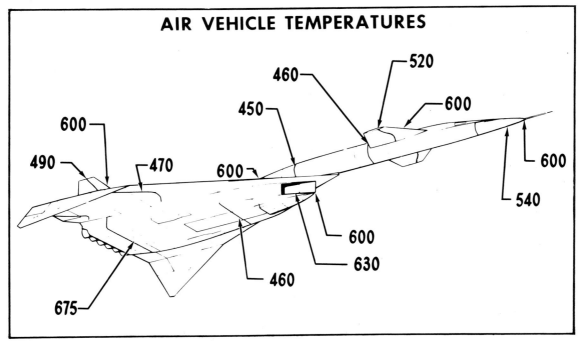

Illustration shows temperatures at various points on XB-70 variable-geometry two-position windshield. Pilots sat 110 feet ahead of the landing gear and about 30 feet up. Fulton said that there was some noise inside the B-70 when windshield was raised or lowered, that with the windshield ramp down, there were some conditions where turbulent air flow around windshield caused cockpit noise. Noise stopped when windshield was raised a few degrees. Rockwell via Schleicher

which houses the engines and twin vertical tails. The nose section of the fuselage contains the radar antenna, navigation equipment, and movable windshield ramp. The crew compartment is environmentally controlled for a shirt sleeve atmosphere and contains completely encapsulating crew escape provisions. The equipment bay with controlled environment is directly behind and accessible from the crew compartment. The canard is supported from this bay. The upper fuselage is cylindrical over much of its length and contains the largest of the many fuel storage tanks. The center fuselage also forms the wing root which together becomes an integral structure to form the air induction system, weapons bay, fuel storage, and support for both the nose and main landing gear. The aft fuselage houses the six engines and supports the twin vertical tails surfaces. The fixed outer wing beyond the root section supports the folding wingtip and four of the six elevon segments. The wingtips fold downward while in supersonic flight and support the remaining two elevon segments. In the original design, both the outer wing and folding tips contained integral fuel tanks, but in the two experimental aircraft no fuel is carried in the tips. Each main landing gear carries a four-wheel bogey and multiple-motion retraction mechanism for storage in the lower center fuselage outboard of the air duct. The dual-wheeled nose gear is located just aft of the apex of the wing root and folds into a cavity between the air ducts. Due to the performance requirements, the aircraft is volume-limited and, consequently maximum utilization is required for fuel storage. The airframe of the XB-70A is unique in many ways. The extraordinary requirements of high-temperature environment, stiffness, thermal protection of the crew, equipment and fuel, volume restriction, and a large expanse of wetted area combined to require a highly redundant structure of varied configurations. The outside surface temperatures existing at Mach 3 cruise made it obvious that aluminum alloy could not be used in the basic structure. Instead, corrosion-resistant steel and titanium became the principal structural materials.

At the nose of the fuselage is a 17x8-foot radome made of high-temperature polyester fibre glass (vibran) which serves as part of the structure. The remaining nose structure, including the movable windshield ramp, is of shell-type titanium construction. The fuselage to the aft bulkhead of the environmental equipment bay is a single-wall titanium shell with H-11 steel longerons, the latter were required for aerolastic stiffness of the forward fuselage supporting the canard surface. The interior of this portion of the fuselage contains a transpiration wall as part of the environmental system and is generally lightly loaded. All factors considered, optimization studies dictated a conventional shell structure consisting of a 6A1-4V titanium outer skin riveted to 4A1-3Mo-1V titanium frames.

Close frame spacing required for equipment support also provided skin panel dimensions that were adequate for surface stiffness. A special part of the windshield structure was the titanium alloy framing required for both strength and stiffness. The main windshield support frame is machined from three titanium forgings flash welded together. For the time period concerned, they represented the largest titanium forgings ever produced.

The remainder of the forward fuselage, which is cylindrical to the apex of the wing, is constructed of PH15-7Mo brazed stainless steel honeycomb reinforced with 17-4PH steel longerons. The governing criteria for this portion of the fuselage were high surface temperatures, insulation for the fuel, high loads, and stiffness requirements. Optimization studies favoring the honeycomb shell was done through the longerons and skin sheer ties at a common bulkhead. Detailed stress analysis augmented by tests of structural components resolved this joining problem.

It is appropriate at this point to describe the canard. The design criteria included very high load levels, high temperature, and extremely rigid stiffness requirements imposed on a 2½ per cent thick airfoil. With no insulation requirements, the canard was designed as a hot structure. The carry-through structure is a narrow box beam made up of front and rear 17-4PH stainless steel spars, two intermediate titanium alloy spars and machined titanium cover panels. The root rib is a 17-4PH stainless steel forging. The fixed portion of the canard outer surface is multicellular. The covers are also sculptured 6A1-4V titanium alloy plates supported by multiple spars and ribs. Both spars and ribs have sine wave webs, burn-through welded to flat flange members. The leading and trailing edges are full-depth brazed honeycomb wedges made from PH15-7Mo steel. The flap likewise has sculptured 6A1-4V titanium skins and corrugated web ribs—the same as for the fixed surface. The entire surface pivots about bearings located at the front spar of the carry-through box beam. Except for the leading and trailing edges and spar assemblies, the covers are attached to the internal structure with mechanical fasteners.

The intermediate fuselage is basically PH15-7Mo brazed steel honeycomb panel construction. The basic reasons for this selection were high temperatures, insulation requirements, fuel containment, high surface loadings, panel and general stiffness requirements. The surface temperatures encountered over the intermediate fuselage are in the vicinity of 460 degrees F over much of the length. This necessitated honeycomb for insulation. The duct walls also required minimum depth supporting structure in the vicinity of the weapons bay and landing gear wells. The high pressure in the integral fuel tanks surrounding the ducts and landing gear bays was an additional reason to use honeycomb.

North American machinists at work on XB-70A components.   Rockwell via Boswell

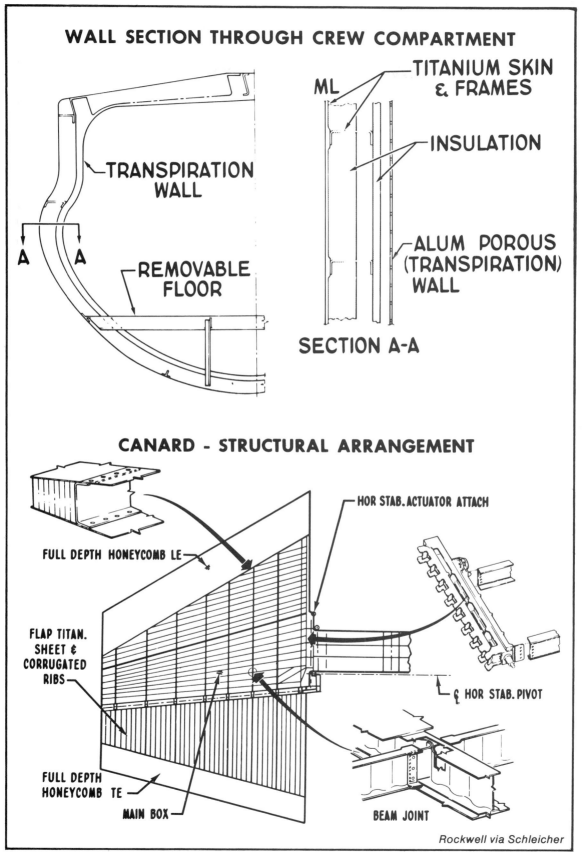

WALL SECTION THROUGH CREW COMPARTMENT

TRANSPIRATION WALL

A — A

REMOVABLE FLOOR

ML

TITANIUM SKIN & FRAMES

INSULATION

ALUM POROUS (TRANSPIRATION) WALL

SECTION A-A

CANARD - STRUCTURAL ARRANGEMENT

HOR STAB. ACTUATOR ATTACH

FULL DEPTH HONEYCOMB LE

FLAP TITAN. SHEET & CORRUGATED RIBS

₡ HOR STAB. PIVOT

FULL DEPTH HONEYCOMB TE

MAIN BOX

BEAM JOINT

Rockwell via Schleicher

37

INTERMEDIATE FUSELAGE - STRUCTURAL ARRANGEMENT

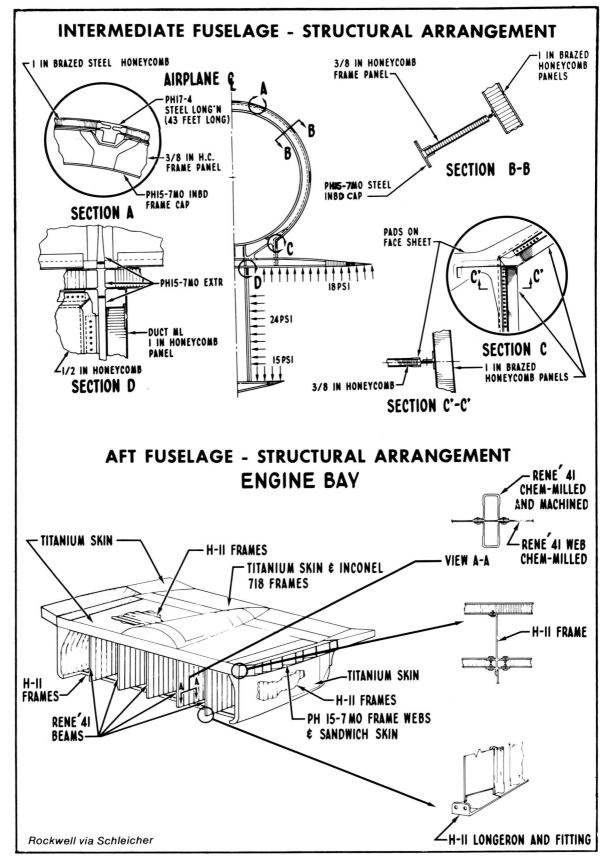

I IN BRAZED STEEL HONEYCOMB

AIRPLANE ₵

PHI7-4 STEEL LONG'N (43 FEET LONG)

3/8 IN H.C. FRAME PANEL

PHI5-7MO INBD FRAME CAP

SECTION A

PHI5-7MO EXTR

DUCT ML I IN HONEYCOMB PANEL

1/2 IN HONEYCOMB

SECTION D

3/8 IN HONEYCOMB FRAME PANEL

I IN BRAZED HONEYCOMB PANELS

SECTION B-B

PHI5-7MO STEEL INBD CAP

18 PSI

24 PSI

15 PSI

PADS ON FACE SHEET

SECTION C

3/8 IN HONEYCOMB

I IN BRAZED HONEYCOMB PANELS

SECTION C'-C'

AFT FUSELAGE - STRUCTURAL ARRANGEMENT
ENGINE BAY

TITANIUM SKIN

H-II FRAMES

TITANIUM SKIN & INCONEL 718 FRAMES

VIEW A-A

RENE' 41 CHEM-MILLED AND MACHINED

RENE' 41 WEB CHEM-MILLED

H-II FRAME

H-II FRAMES

RENE' 41 BEAMS

TITANIUM SKIN

H-II FRAMES

PH 15-7 MO FRAME WEBS & SANDWICH SKIN

H-II LONGERON AND FITTING

Rockwell via Schleicher

WING - STRUCTURAL DETAILS

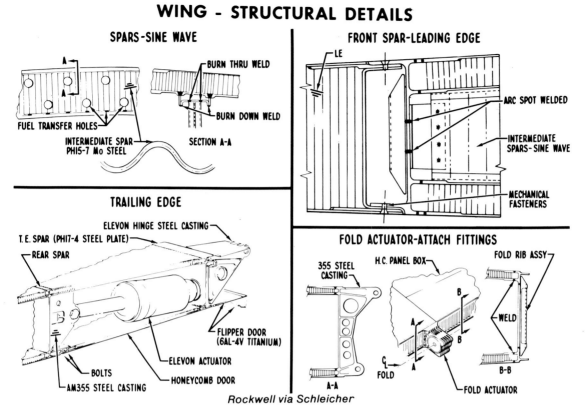

SPARS-SINE WAVE

BURN THRU WELD

BURN DOWN WELD

FUEL TRANSFER HOLES

INTERMEDIATE SPAR PHI5-7 Mo STEEL

SECTION A-A

FRONT SPAR-LEADING EDGE

LE

ARC SPOT WELDED

INTERMEDIATE SPARS-SINE WAVE

MECHANICAL FASTENERS

TRAILING EDGE

ELEVON HINGE STEEL CASTING

T. E. SPAR (PHI7-4 STEEL PLATE)

REAR SPAR

FLIPPER DOOR (6AL-4V TITANIUM)

ELEVON ACTUATOR

BOLTS

HONEYCOMB DOOR

AM355 STEEL CASTING

FOLD ACTUATOR-ATTACH FITTINGS

355 STEEL CASTING

H.C. PANEL BOX

FOLD RIB ASSY

WELD

FOLD

B-B

A-A

FOLD ACTUATOR

Rockwell via Schleicher

During the design of the air ducts and movable duct panels, it became necessary to limit the wall deflections to minute values so as not to impair the control of the shock waves. This necessitated panels having extreme stiffness in all directions, and honeycomb panels met this criteria.

There was a departure from honeycomb in the design of the frames passing over the main air ducts. This space constitutes a secondary duct for boundary-layer bleed air. Sheet metal frames were replaced with truss type webs. These were welded and heat-treated H-11 steel tube trusses which attached through cap fittings located in the wing upper cover and main duct honeycomb panels. In the intermediate fuselage, the remaining internal framing consisted of honeycomb panels and beaded web frames. Longitudinal strength was achieved through the high in-plane strength of the honeycomb panels augmented by steel longerons located in strategic locations. Due to the high stiffness of steel honeycomb panels, there was little shear lag in distributing in-plane loads to adjacent panels or longerons. This was especially true in the vicinity of the landing gear attachment, where very high concentrated loads occurred. The longerons for the most part were 17-4PH steel. All assembly, except for the bolted-in

trusses, was done by welding and to varying degrees included all types. The predominant type, however, was machine tungsten inert gas (TIG) welding.

The aft fuselage can best be described as a hybrid structure consisting of various materials and types of construction. The design criteria were most severe. The external skin temperatures range up to 675 degrees F whereas the internal framing reached 920 degrees F due to engine heat. Since the engines occupy most of the internal volume of this portion of the fuselage, no full depth transverse framing could exist for a length of approximately 26 feet. In order to carry the wing bending loads across this part of the fuselage, multiple shallow depth crossbeams form the upper part of large bents. The side and lower transverse frames supporting hinged engine access doors are used to complete the bent. The spars were stiffened flat titanium alloy webs with H-11 steel caps riveted thereto. The side frames were machined from H-11 bar with titanium webs and bolted to the upper crossbeams. At the side of the fuselage, the honeycomb sandwich wing stub was joined to the H-11 frames to rough high-strength mechanical fasteners. The skin covering over the top and sides was 6A1-4V titanium alloy riveted to the web. The engine compartment hinged doors were of typical sheet metal construction using 6A1-4V titanium skins and 4A1-3Mo-1V titanium framing.

The twin vertical tail surfaces are supported by the aft fuselage previously described. These were all-movable thin airfoils hinged about a 45 degrees axis to the supporting structure. The supporting base is multispar with honeycomb panels attached by mechanical fasteners to the wing root juncture with the aft fuselage. The vertical tails are multi-spar with thin brazed steel honeycomb sandwich panels riveted together. The spars are sine wave webs, burn-through welded to flat caps and are made from 6A1-4V titanium. The leading and trailing edges are brazed steel full-depth honeycomb wedges.

The wing is composed of a fixed portion permanently attached to the stub and a deflecting outer panel. It is a multispar design with brazed steel honeycomb sandwich cover panels and full depth honeycomb leading edges. The spars are sine wave webs, burn-through welded to flat flanges. Between the front and rear spars, the fixed wing structure constitutes integral fuel tankage. The movable wingtip is mounted to the fixed wing by means of six hydraulic-powered rotary actuators having a gear reduction ratio of 32,000-to-1. These are pin-connected to AM-355 steel hinge castings which, in turn, are permanently welded to the wing cover panels. Immediately aft of the rear spar is a compartment which contains the elevon actuators and these are accessible through bolted-on honeycomb doors in the lower surface. AM-355 stainless steel castings are used as elevon hinges and actuator supports and are welded into the basic structure. The elevons consist of a spar with thin honeycomb sandwich cover panels and a full depth honeycomb trailing edge.

As for the main landing gear, a four-wheel axle-beam is supported from the lower fork of the oleo strut and pivots in a pitch mode. A compensating and folding actuator controls the pitching of the axle-beam and oleo piston about a vertical axis. Thus, for retraction, the axle-beam is first pitched downward so that its fore-and-aft axis became parallel to the axis of the oleo strut, then rotated almost 90-degrees about the strut and subsequently retracted aft into the wheel well. The gear in its entirety was constructed of H-11 steel heat-treated to 280 to 300 ksi. The nose gear is conventional in most respects. It retracts aft with a single motion into the nose gear well. A pair of corotating wheels are supported directly from the lower end of the shock

strut. A single drag brace is used, and torque is reacted directly through the upper trunnion fitting. A steering mechanism and towing provisions are included. The nose gear, like the main gear, is constructed of H-11 steel heat-treated to 280 to 300 ksi.

From the foregoing descriptions, it will be noted that a variety of structural configurations and materials were employed in the airframe of the XB-70. Many optimization studies were made prior to final selection in each case. The severity of the design criteria, and stiffness requirements in addition to space, volume, and weight limitations, played a major role in the design. The result was a multi-path or redundant structural arrangement which was contributed greatly to a damage tolerant design. Normal pressure loadings were particularly severe for all parts of the structure. These included cabin pressures, sonic disturbances, and fuel tank inerting pressures. Practically all panels of the 22,000 square feet of honeycomb sandwich used were critical for both high inplane loads and normal pressures. Thus, the allowable strength of each panel had to be determined for systems of combined loadings. The inherent stiffness of brazed steel honeycomb sandwich minimized the amount of internal supporting structure required. Welded joints likewise saved a large penalty in structural weight over conventional mechanical fasteners. The venture into an entirely new form of construction with new materials and newly developed processes presented one of the greatest challenges to structural engineers of the 1960s.

The strucutural design of the XB-70 exhibits extraordinary design. Not only were the structural problems severe, but from basic materials to finished product, very little resembling past experience remained applicable. New analytical methods were formulated and much testing was done to verify the basic approaches. New standards were established and new hardware designed and qualified to replace the old.

A new relationship between Manufacturing, Engineering, and Quality Assurance was established, which made this triumvirate an inseparable team during the course of fabrication and assembly. There exists today an established materials review procedure more complete both in magnitude and inventiveness from what came before. Dispositions were frequently preceded by experimentation and/or research.

The physical size and weight of the XB-70

placed it ahead of contemporary aircraft and made it the forerunner of things to come. The XB-70's structural design and construction successes were demonstrated in its flight test program, especially during one 32 minute sustained Mach 3 flight.

In all respects, it can be concluded that in design and construction, the XB-70 represented a state of the art for manned aircraft."

Fuselage

The B-70's fuselage was of semi-monocoque (type of construction which relies on the outer skin to carry the stress) structure of basic circular section, changing to a flat-top section in the crew cabin area. It was constructed mainly of titanium alloys forward of its wing and of brazed stainless steel honeycomb sandwich panels over the wing. The nose radome was manufactured of laminated Vibran. The fuselage featured area-rule (reduced frontal cross section area of the fuselage where pinching-in the waist minimized the difference between flight velocity and localized airflow velocities) to improve upon its transonic performance. The design of the fuselage suggested that it was to act as an airfoil in itself. Housed within the B-70's fuselage were many items, a few of which are listed below:
- Five integral fuel tanks and related equipment
- Two-man (flight test), four-man (operational) crew cabin
- Radio and related electronic equipment
- Recording systems, digital and analog-type computers
- Flight control system and related electronics; recording gear; gust recorder
- Cabin air system
- Ammonia and water tanks
- Parachute braking system with three 28-foot diameter parachutes
- Environmental control system
- Avionics system; offensive and defensive (operational only) electronics
- Air conditioning system
- Radar and related equipment
- Emergency escape systems; blast doors and escape hatches
- Variable-geometry, two-position windshield and ramp assembly
- Port side crew entry door
- Electronics equipment bay
- Inflight refueling receptacle

Wing, Wingtips and Elevon Control Surfaces

The B-70 wing spanned 105 feet with its folding wingtips raised. The entire wing surface (upper and lower) was covered with brazed stainless steel honeycomb sandwich panels, welded together. The leading edges were honeycomb sandwich attached directly to the front spar (a structural member of the wing that carries the largest portion of the stresses). The spars were of the sine-wave webbed type. The wing was cantilever (a structure without external support in which all stresses are carried within) delta-wing (a triangular planform type wing) of very thin section with anhedral (a downward angle of a wing or stabilizer with respect to the lateral axis) over its entire span with a slight washout aerodynamic twist (a lesser angle of incidence to decrease lift; variation of the zero-lift line along the span of a wing or other airfoil). On the other hand, XB-70A-2 featured a 5 degrees dihedral (an upward angle of a wing or stabilizer) with respect ratio (ratio of the wing span to the wing chord—a reference line on an airfoil extending from the leading edge to the trailing edge) of 1.751 with a chord of 117.9-feet at the root, 2.2¼ feet at the tip.

The B-70 wing was large and complicated. It not only served as a basic lifting device, but also as a huge integral fuel tank. It featured folding variable-geometry wingtips each about the size of a B-58's wing, 12 elevon control surfaces, six integral fuel tanks, 24 elevon actuators, 12 wingtip power hinges with motors, and miles of electrical wiring, flight control cables, fuel pumps and lines, hydraulic tubing and related equipment. In the original design, both outer wingtips were to contain additional fuel tanks; in the two prototypes, however, no tanks were installed in the wingtips. If the B-70 had gone into production, this particular feature may have been applied.

B-70 wingtips were folded downward hydraulically during flight to improve both high speed stability and maneuverability. For low altitude supersonic flight the wingtips were lowered to an angle of 25 degrees (mid-down position) and for high altitude M3 cruise the wingtips were lowered to their full-down position of 65 degrees.

The downward twist or conical camber of the wing's leading edge aided subsonic performance, whereas the folding wingtips enhanced lift for transonic and supersonic flight. The B-70's variable-geometry wingtips allowed the use of shorter vertical fins, as the wingtips provided excellent stability and a notable reduction in drag. In fact, if the B-70 wingtips had been fixed, the twin vertical fins would have required twice as much area and weight; 467.92 square feet versus 233.96 sq. ft. as used.

Each B-70 wingtip comprised almost 500 sq. ft. and was folded downward by six Curtiss-Wright 32,000-to-1 hinge motors housed under black magnesium thorium fairings which formed the wingtip hinge lines. By moving the wingtips downward, the generated lift aft of the center of gravity was reduced, appreciably minimizing trip correction demands from the canard flap surfaces. Effectual wing area near the trailing edge was reduced as the tips lowered, consequently shifting net lift forward, closer to the craft's CG. A marvel associated with supersonic flight is dealt with in this manner; by reducing the area near the trailing edge, wing lift moves forward instead of aft. Therefore, to reduce the need for trim and to effectively cut drag, the aerodynamic center, or center of pressure should be as close to the aircraft's CG as possible.

Each B-70 wing had six elevon control surfaces which moved in unison for both aerodynamic control and trim. As the wingtip moved downward, the two outboard elevons locked parallel to the tip panel, forming a fixed surface. The tips, designed for lateral (side-to-side) control and longitudinal (end-to-end) stability,

Shown are XB-70A main landing gear oleos. Each oleo was constructed from machined, heat-treated H-11 steel to 280–300 ksi. Note forward and aft trunnion braces. Cleveland Pneumatic

MAIN LANDING GEAR - STRUCTURAL ARRANGEMENT

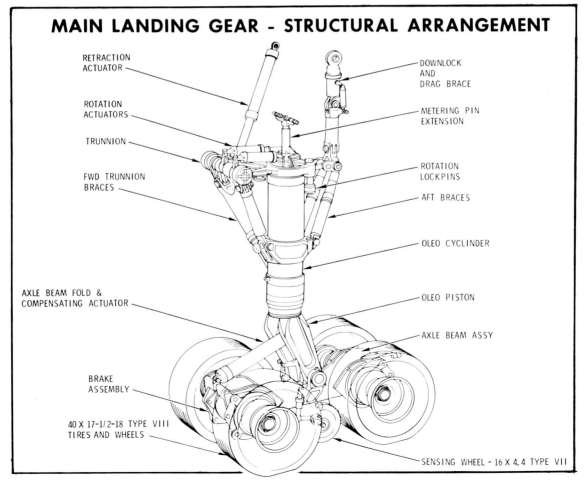

RETRACTION ACTUATOR

ROTATION ACTUATORS

TRUNNION

FWD TRUNNION BRACES

AXLE BEAM FOLD & COMPENSATING ACTUATOR

BRAKE ASSEMBLY

40 X 17-1/2-18 TYPE VIII TIRES AND WHEELS

DOWNLOCK AND DRAG BRACE

METERING PIN EXTENSION

ROTATION LOCKPINS

AFT BRACES

OLEO CYCLINDER

OLEO PISTON

AXLE BEAM ASSY

SENSING WHEEL - 16 X 4.4 TYPE VII

"VALKYRIE"

NORTH AMERICAN

XB-70A

SUPERSONIC BOMBER

LEGEND

1. DRAG CHUTE COMPARTMENT
2. FLAP (CANARD)
3. GROUND ESCAPE HATCH
4. ESCAPE CAPSULE HATCHES
5. ENGINE BY-PASS BLEED DOORS
6. RUDDER HINGE LINE

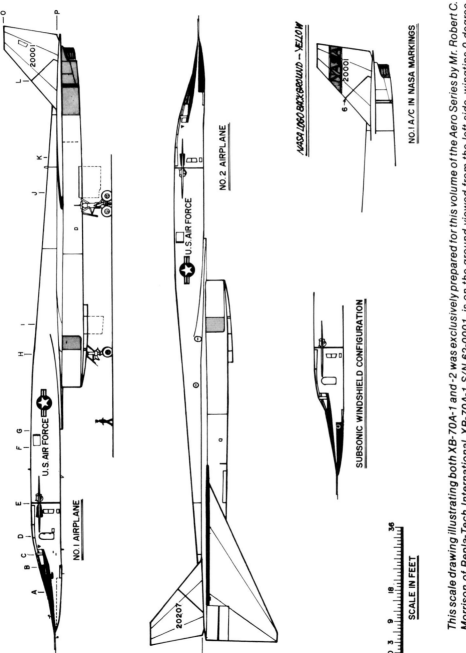

NASA LOGO BACKGROUND — YELLOW

20001

6

NO. I A/C IN NASA MARKINGS

NO. I AIRPLANE

U.S. AIR FORCE

20001

NO. 2 AIRPLANE

U.S. AIR FORCE

SUBSONIC WINDSHIELD CONFIGURATION

20207

SCALE IN FEET

0 3   9   18   36

This scale drawing illustrating both XB-70A-1 and -2 was exclusively prepared for this volume of the Aero Series by Mr. Robert C. Morrison of Repla-Tech International. XB-70A-1 S/N 62-0001, is on the ground viewed from the left side, wingtips 0 degree. XB-70A-2 S/N 62-0207, is shown in clean, high-supersonic flight configuration, wingtips full-down (65 degrees), viewed from the right side. Note that ship No. 2's lower radome is painted black, unlike ship No. 1. The bottom, top and front views show XB-70A-1 after the "exiter," or "shaker" vanes were installed to induce turbulence. Both of the full side views show the windshield in super-sonic flight configuration, whereas the partial side view depicts XB-70A-2 with subsonic configuration, and the other partial side view shows XB-70A-1 with NASA logo on its vertical fin which has a yellow background. In addition, a scale bar, cross-section reference, color code and legend is provided. Cross-section reference shows the fuselage, wing, canard and vertical stabilizer.

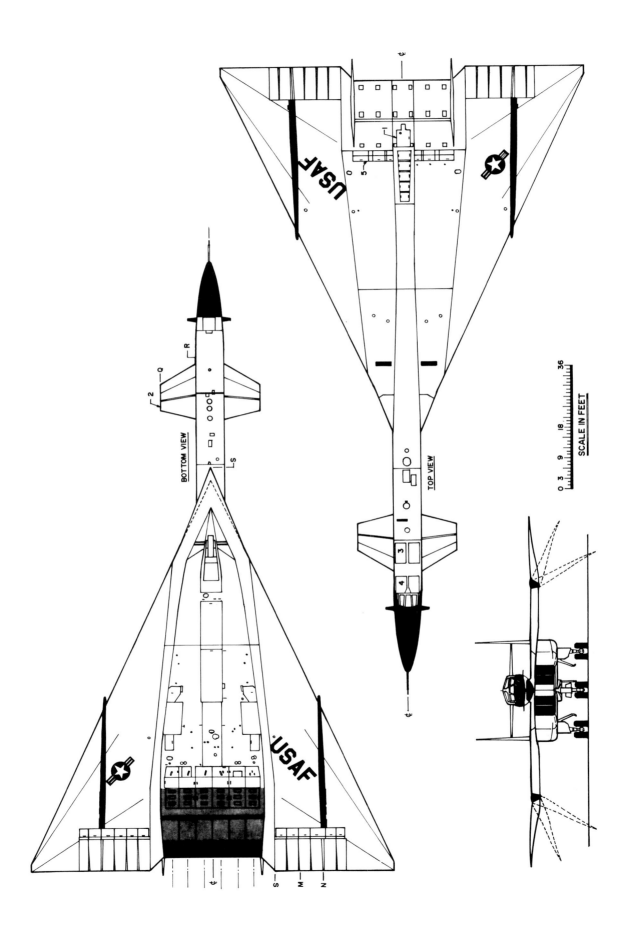

BOTTOM VIEW

USAF

TOP VIEW

USAF

SCALE IN FEET

0 3 9 18 36

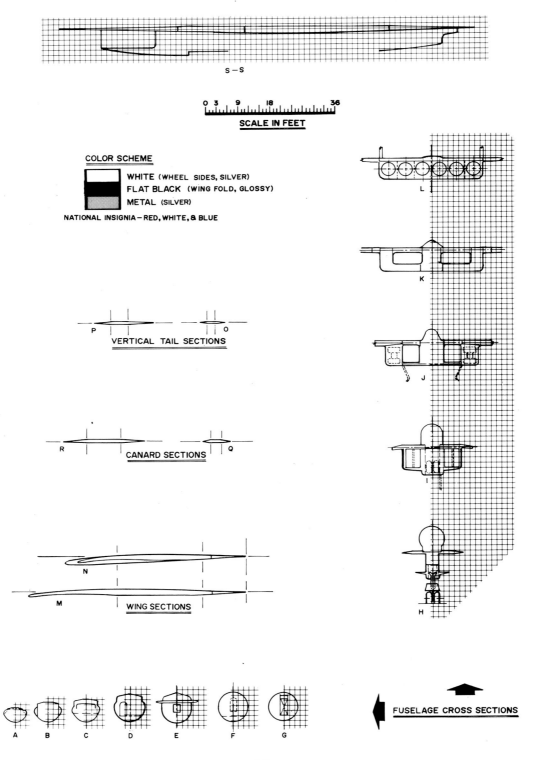

S — S

0 3 9 18 36
SCALE IN FEET

COLOR SCHEME

WHITE (WHEEL SIDES, SILVER)
FLAT BLACK (WING FOLD, GLOSSY)
METAL (SILVER)
NATIONAL INSIGNIA — RED, WHITE, & BLUE

P   O
VERTICAL TAIL SECTIONS

R   Q
CANARD SECTIONS

N
M
WING SECTIONS

L

K

J

I

H

A   B   C   D   E   F   G

FUSELAGE CROSS SECTIONS

46

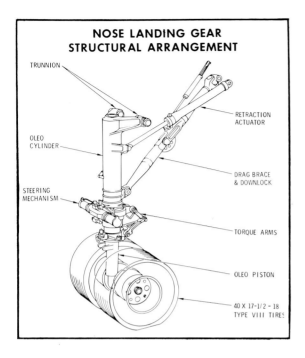

NOSE LANDING GEAR STRUCTURAL ARRANGEMENT

TRUNNION

RETRACTION ACTUATOR

OLEO CYLINDER

DRAG BRACE & DOWNLOCK

STEERING MECHANISM

TORQUE ARMS

OLEO PISTON

40 X 17-1/2 - 18 TYPE VIII TIRES

offered an additional 5% lift when in full-down configuration. By reason of design, the tips worked in conjunction with the B-70's splitter plate and the wedge shape of its underbelly to provide this additional lift. When full-down, the shock wave generated by the tips whirlpooled to the underside of the B-70's wing, adding to its overall compression lift profile. With the tips straight and level, the two outboard elevons were operational, thereby allowing all 12 elevons to work in conjunction with the canard flaps to raise the B-70's nose to the favored 9

degrees angle of attack for both takeoff and landing. Elevon travel is 30 degrees up, 30 degrees down.

Vertical Stabilizer, Rudder

The B-70 featured the use of twin vertical stabilizers which doubled as large area angle-hinged rudders of construction similar to that of the wings. The rudders were controlled by hydraulic actuators, each powered by two independent hydraulic fluid systems. The sweepback angle on the vertical fin's leading edge was 51 degrees, and the total area was 233.96 sq. ft.

Canard Foreplane

A notable feature in the B-70's configuration was its canard foreplane. A canard is a short, stubby, wing-like element on an aircraft forward of its wing and CG, which provides increased pitch stability. The canard offered a long moment arm forward of the B-70's center of gravity so that trim deflections of the canard could be notably less than with elevons or elevators. The moment of the resultant force on the wing is the product of the force and the distance from the line of action of the force to the point about which the moment is taken; moments which act in a manner tending to increase the angle of attack are called stalling moments and are designated by a positive sign; moments which tend to decrease the angle of attack are called friving moments and are negative in sign; thus, B-70's canard provided increased lift. It is an established fact that critical instability occurs at transonic

STRUCTURAL TESTS - MAJOR SPECIMENS

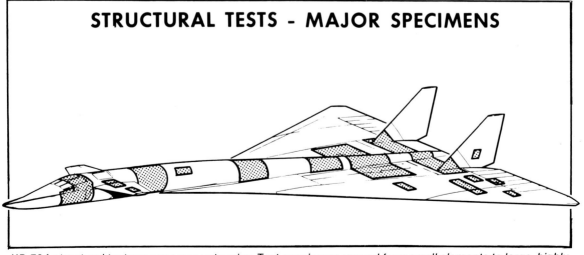

XB-70A structural test program was extensive. Test specimens ranged from small elements to large, highly redundant assemblies. Sixteen major component tests were conducted representing airframe.
Rockwell via Schleicher

GENERAL ARRANGEMENT

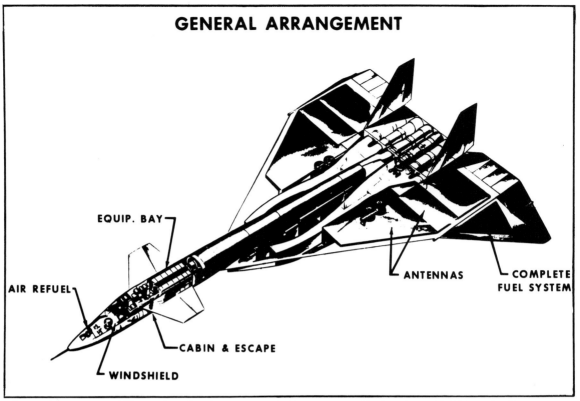

EQUIP. BAY

AIR REFUEL

CABIN & ESCAPE

WINDSHIELD

ANTENNAS

COMPLETE FUEL SYSTEM

General arrangement illustration showing proposed wingtip internal fuel tanks and inflight refuelling receptacle. Note electronic equipment bay between canards.   *Rockwell via Schleicher*

MATERIALS USED IN THE XB-70

TITANIUM - CONVENTIONAL STRUCTURE

STEEL SANDWICH (PH 15-7 Mo)

H-II STEEL - CONVENTIONAL STRUCTURE

NICKEL BASE ALLOY - CONVENTIONAL STRUCTURE

RADOME

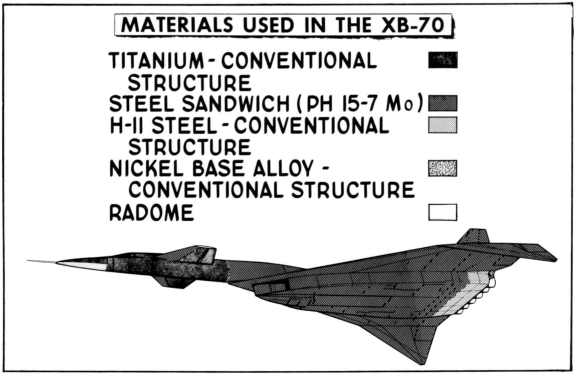

Materials distribution of XB-70. Built mostly of stainless steel honeycomb sandwich panels, XB-70s were also constructed of titanium, H-11 steel, and nickel base alloys. Radome was made of high-temperature polyester fibre glass, is called Vibran.   *Rockwell via Schleicher*

She was big, sleek and beautiful—and, a sight to see. Though several years behind schedule, her roll-out on May 11, 1964, was a spellbinding occasion. It was a big moment for American aeronautical achievement. The Valkyrie had arrived.   *Rockwell via Gene Boswell*

XB-70A-1 being towed out from her parking area for yet another flight test. Before retirement, A/V-1 demonstrated her abilities 83 times. She now sits out a lonely vigil at the Air Force Museum near Dayton, Ohio. Note A/V-2 in the background.   *Rockwell via Gene Boswell*

Aft view of XB-70A-1 at the U.S. Air Force Museum near Dayton, Ohio, where it is displayed today. Note size of exhaust nozzles and protective, see-through plexiglass covers.　　　　　　　　*Detail and Scale via Bert Kinzey*

XB-70A-1 with its six J93s blazing during an engine runup at Edwards. Each engine was rated in the 30,000 lb. thrust class for a total output exceeding 180,000 pounds. Note NASA's logo on vertical fin.
Rockwell via Gene Boswell

While a Northrop T-38 Talon flies chase, XB-70A-1 takes a test hop over the Mojave Desert. Note that A/V-1's variable-geometry wingtips are at zero degrees deflection.   *Rockwell via Gene Boswell*

Rotating, XB-70A-2 begins its inital flight test from Palmdale, California. After both low- and high-speed handling characteristics were evaluated, she joined her sister ship at Edwards. Before she was downed on June 8, 1966, she tookoff another 45 times.   *Rockwell via Gene Boswell*

During her initial flight test, XB-70A-2 was evaluated for both low- and high-speed handling characteristics. Here, she is shown during the low-speed segment.   *Rockwell via Gene Boswell*

Here, XB-70A-2 is shown during her high-speed evaluation with wingtips mid-down (25 degrees). Before she landed at Edwards, Mach 1-plus was achieved.

Rockwell via Gene Boswell

Copilot's station in XB-70A-1. Instrument panels were illuminated with white light, a visibility improvement over customary red lighting. Note large fuel management display left of control yoke.

Detail & Scale via Bert Kinzey

Pilot's station in XB-70A-1. Positional indicators were designed on realistic terms, (i.e., altitude was shown on a vertical scale rather than the conventional circular type of clock instrumentation). Additionally, all eleven fuel tanks were individually represented on a tape-type display panel.   *Detail & Scale via Bert Kinzey*

A fifth wheel was incorporated to prevent skidding and tire blowouts, this wheel can be seen between the main wheels and wheel chocks. The entire landing gear system was subjected to severe heating at M3 cruise. In action, the BF Goodrich tires, which were treated with a special, heat-resistant silver paint, were designed to operate at temperatures up to 360 degrees F. Each of the main gear bogies (shown) had four, load-carrying wheels, while the nose gear had two.   *Detail & Scale via Bert Kinzey*

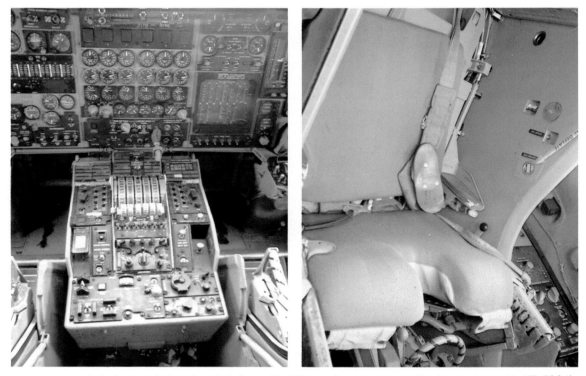

Center console between pilot and copilot shows throttle quadrant and central instrument panel in XB-70A-1. Photo on right shows pilot's seat. Note encapsulation ring between thigh supports.

Detail & Scale via Bert Kinzey

B-70s featured a large foreplane or canard which mounted aft of cockpit and crew entry door. Canard spanned 28.8 feet, came with large flaps. Photo on right shows B-70's twin vertical stabilizers which doubled as rudders. Note that B-70 is parked nose-to-nose with a B-52.   *Detail & Scale via Bert Kinzey*

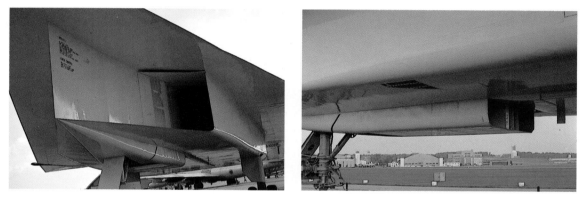

Photo on left shows XB-70A-1's left rectangular, 65x47 inch variable geometry air inlet with boundary layer bleed slot; intake tunnels were about 80 feet long and 7 feet high at the duct end. Photo on right shows nose landing gear, its streamlined housing.   *Detail & Scale via Bert Kinzey*

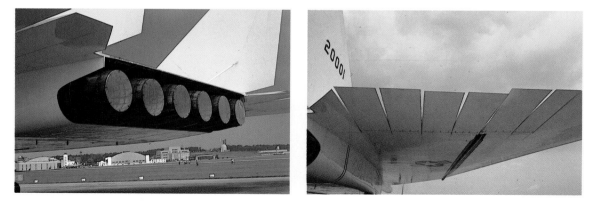

XB-70A-1's six J93 exhaust nozzles which featured fully-variable, converging-diverging openings. Photo on right illustrates the six elevons on XB-70A-1's right (starboard) wing; the two outer elevons locked during wingtip deflections downward.   *Detail & Scale via Bert Kinzey*

TB-58A Hustler, XB-70A-2 approaching an Edwards AFB runway after a sonic boom flight test. B-70's v-g wingtips were nearly as large as B-58's entire wing.   *Rockwell via Boswell*

XB-70A-1 and TB-58A return to Edwards AFB after sonic boom test flight.   *Rockwell via Bear*

XB-70A-1 during 4th flight test, its wingtips were lowered to mid-down the first time. Note engine bleed air bypass doors atop wings over engine bays.   *Rockwell*

XB-70A-2 in hangar four days before roll-out which occurred 29 May 1965. Workmen are testing its wing-fold mechanisms; wing-tips were lowered from zero to 65 degrees full-down during these tests. Note that XB-70 is on jacks for wingtip to floor clearance.
Rockwell

speeds (600-to-800 mph; through or near the region of Mach 1—the speed of sound) when the center of pressure (CP) moves aft the movements can be countered by trimming with an elevon control surface, but the ensuing higher AOA increases drag. With a canard foreplane, however, the AOA is increased to counter CP shift without altering the AOA of the wing.

On the B-70, the aft portion of the canard was hinged by hydraulic actuators, each powered by two independent hydraulic fluid systems to lower, or deflect through 25 degrees, forming a conventional flap. When the canard flap was drooped at low approach speed, the B-70 nose pitched up. The resulting change in trim (balance of the aircraft) was compensated for by moving the control column forward, drooping the elevons, which worked in conjunction with the canard flaps. At that point, maximum lift was achieved and nothing was subtracted from primary wing lift. Thus, the landing atti-

tude was shallower and the L/D ratio was higher—permitting landing speeds comparable, in North American's view, to jet-powered commercial airliners.

The canard foreplane was located on the B-70 fuselage just aft of the flight deck and crew entry door. It was used primarily for both lift control and trim change during supersonic flight. It also played an important role in takeoff and landing of the big plane. It featured an all-movable main surface with, as mentioned earlier, a trailing edge flap. The canard was linked directly to the 12 trailing edge, wing-mounted elevons and, as the elevons moved

through minus 25 to plus 15 degrees, the canard flap surface deflected from zero to 6 degrees. Canard stall occurred below MO.88, causing severe airframe buffeting. For takeoff and landing, the canard's main section was set at 0 degrees incidence while its flap surface was deflected downward to provide maximum lift at the nose.

The B-70 canard foreplane's leading edge sweepback angle was 31.70 degrees with an aspect ratio of 1.997 and a total area, including the fuselage portion, of 415.59 sq. ft. (265.28 sq. ft. excluding the fuselage portion). The span was 28.81 feet.

XB-70A-1 had slight anhedral over its entire wing span, whereas XB-70A-2 featured 5 degrees dihedral. Twin vertical stabilizers were all-moving, doubled as rudders. Leading edge sweepback of vertical fins was 51° 46', both hinged about a 45 degree axis to stationary support structures; rudder travel was 12 degrees maximum left to right. XB-70A-1 is shown.   *Rockwell*

Artists impression of XB-70A released in 1963. Note SAC band aft of canards.   *Rockwell*

North American's canard design was largely attributable to the overall aerodynamic success of the B-70; however, the design was not invented by them. The Wright Flyer of 1903 was of canard design. Moreover, H.C. Barber of England built a canard in 1913 (which he called Valkyrie). The word canard is from the French, meaning duck, and applied to the neck-like projection forward of a wing.

Exiter Vane

During the joint USAF-NASA flight test phase, an exiter or shaker vane was installed on XB-70A number 1. This winglet was mounted to induce turbulence in a series of tests of the sophisticated elastic mode control system called ILAF (Identically Located Acceleration and Force).

During ILAF tests, this exiter or shaker vane induced oscillations in the aircraft's structure of from 1 to 8 cycles per second during supersonic flight. ILAF dampers smoothed these out. ILAF tests were conducted throughout the summer and fall of 1968. A similar vane is used to counter turbulence of Rockwell's B-1.

B-70 SYSTEMS

Environmental Control System

Because of the searing friction encountered on the B-70's outer skins while cruising at 2,000 miles per hour and at an altitude exceeding 12 miles, the B-70 generated and absorbed enough heat during a normal flight to maintain a 150 room hotel for 80 hours. To keep its crew from roasting, the B-70's environmental control system cooled the cockpit to a constant 70 to 80 degrees F. Shirt-sleeve comfort prevailed not only in the crew cabin, but in the aircraft's electronics bay where crewmen could make inflight repairs if required, greatly enhancing the reliability of the electronic gear.

Despite altitudes higher than 70,000 feet crewmen needed no cumbersome oxygen masks or pressure suits because the environmental control system provided an atmospheric pressure equal to that of 8,000 feet.

For cooling, the XB-70A aircraft featured a "transpiration wall," a method used by North American to cool the crew cabin walls and provide internal water circulation. Actual tests conducted on a full size crew compartment mock-up, demonstrated that this structural method of cooling proved more efficient than any concept.

Cabin cooling and pressurization within the B-70 was provided by a bleed air/Freon refrigeration/pressurization subsystem. Dual Freon (an odorless gas) refrigeration units were used in parallel to form a continuous air loop, providing both cooling a pressurization for the cockpit and electronic equipment bay.

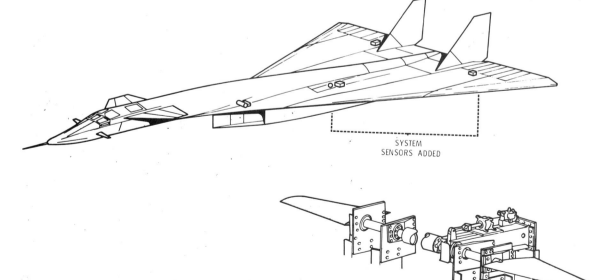

SYSTEM SENSORS ADDED

SHAKER VANE

During the later phase of the B-70's flight test program, a shaker or exiter vane was fitted to XB-70A-1 for evaluation. The application of this vane induced turbulence in a series of tests, coupled with its elastic mode control system called ILAF (identically located acceleration and force). These vanes induced oscillations in the aircraft's structure from 1 to 8 cycles per second during supersonic flight. Onboard ILAF dampers smoothed these varying cycles out. These tests were conducted throughout the summer and fall of 1968. Today, a similar vane is fitted to Rockwell's B-1 to counter turbulence. Rockwell

In the event of sudden decompression, two ram-air doors in the fuselage could have allowed outside air to repressurize the crew cabin. Engine bleed air at high pressure and about 850 degrees F. was ducted into the cooling units to drive the Freon compressor turbines. Additional bleed air for cabin repressurization and cooling egressed the Freon-cooled heat exchanger at about 40 degrees F. A series of tiny holes perforated the walls in the areas that required cooling.

Cockpit and electronics bay air was vacuumed into the glass-lined plenum chamber aft of the transpiration wall and routed back into the freon heat exchanger following its passage through the water-vaporizer heat exchanger. A large cylindrical tank was located behind the cockpit area and contained the water supply used by the vaporizer. Another similar tank housed liquid ammonia to provide an auxiliary supply for use following long duration flights as the primary water tank emptied.

The plenum chamber was insulated from the 470° F outer skin by 2 inches of glass wool on the inside surface of the skin, a dead air gap, and a thinner glass wool layer that maintained inner surface temperatures of about 150° F. During the cooling cycle, crew cabin air heated 90° to 100° F following its emergence from the refrigeration system. In that temperature range, the air flowed through the 102° F transpiration wall at a rate of .21 pounds per minute per square foot. Before recycling through the heat exchangers, cooling air flowed through the plenum chamber, increasing to a temperature of about 114° F. That allowed the temperature within the cockpit to stabilize at 70° F to 80° F, and permitted the electronics bay to maintain at temperatures of 130° F to 160° F. Both the fuel and water heat-exchangers were located in fuel tank number 3 (center fuselage tank) which provided cooling for the "water walls" surrounding various compartments, such as the landing gear wells and braking parachute enclosure.

The B-70 structure was designed to withstand sudden decompression. Like the cockpit and electronics bay, the emergency escape system modules could be pressurized to allow the crew safe exit or landing in the event of an emergency situation. Once closed, they automatically pressurized to equal an altitude of 8,000 feet.

Full-scale XB-70A crew cabin mockup underwent environmental heat chamber tests. Tests measured exterior skin temperatures and inside crew cabin temperatures as well. GE heat lamps were used to simulate external skin temperatures of 1,000 degrees F.
Rockwell

Both XB-70A prototype aircraft featured a two-man test crew: pilot and copilot. However, the YB-70B production prototype and the planned production B-70s would have been manned by a crew of four: pilot, copilot, bombardier-navigator, and electronic countermeasure officer. Each would have required a good escape system.

Emergency Escape System

For the B-70, North American devised a capsule-type ejection seat system. It was modeled to allow the crewmen to operate safely at 70,000 to 80,000 foot heights, and more importantly to safely escape the aircraft in a dire emergency. The capsule could be launched via rocket-propulsion anywhere from zero to 80,000 feet.

The cocoon-like capsule provided for each crew member formed by closure of its upper and lower clamshell doors. Each capsule featured self-contained pressurization and oxygen systems to protect the crewman, becoming a secondary sealed enclosure in the event of sudden decompression.

Trim knobs located within the capsule would

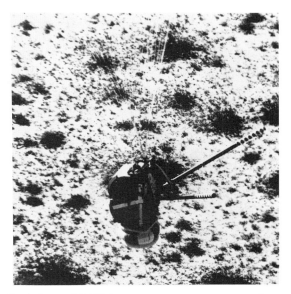

Test drop of B-70 type emergency escape system capsule. Note its air-filled rubber abative bag has deployed to cushion landing shock. The two long booms provided stability during descent. Impact bladder did not deploy on White's capsule 8 June 1966, and he sustained back and internal organ injuries when his capsule impacted at an estimated force of 43 Gs. Rockwell

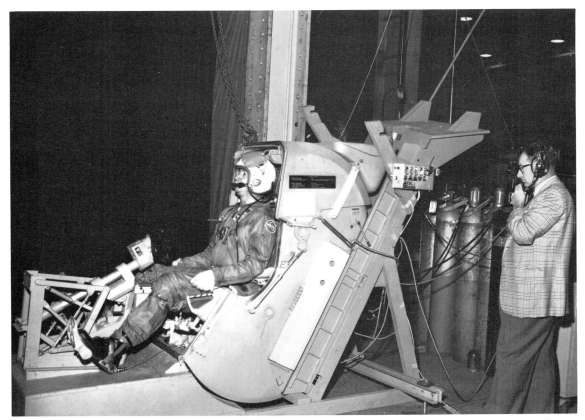

Al White during emergency escape test. Note White's hand pulling lever to initiate encapsulation. Experience gained here saved his life later.
Rockwell via Boswell

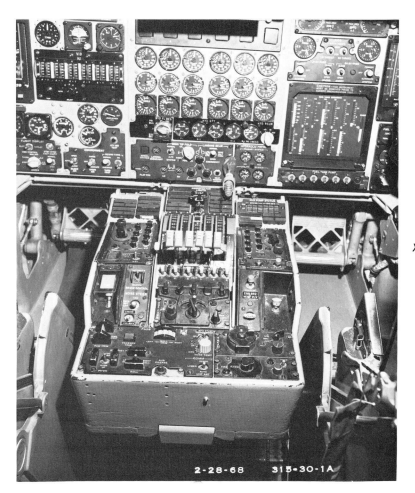

XB-70A-1 Cockpit details.
Rockwell via Boswell

2-28-68   315-30-1A

allow its rider to control the B-70 while descent to a lower altitude was made. The GE J93 engine throttles could be retarded but not advanced from inside the capsule. Providing throttle advance capabilities within the electromechanical remote system employed by the B-70 would have added to its cost and complexity.

A window in the forward part of the capsule would enable the crewmen to monitor the aircraft's flight instrumentation while descending. At lower altitudes the clamshell doors could be retracted allowing the pilot to regain full control. Each capsule featured self-contained pressurization and oxygen systems to protect the crewmen, becoming a secondary sealed enclosure in the event of sudden decompression. To position the B-70 pilot or copilot properly before closure of the clamshell doors, the seat reclined backward about 20 degrees to begin encapsulation. The heels of the crewman had to be positioned in detents before the ejection sequence could proceed.

If the B-70 crewmen elected to eject after the doors were properly closed, they activated another control lever which would automatically jettison the upper fuselage escape hatch panels and clamshell blast doors, then fire the capsule up and away from the doomed plane. The closed and ejected capsule's rocket motor burnout would come at 0.5 seconds, with a trajectory peak of plus 325 feet at 1.9 seconds. Its descent chute would deploy automatically at 9 seconds (about 15,000 feet) followed by a 28 feet-per-second descent and landing. The capsule was aerodynamically stabilized by two booms. The capsule featured an automatically inflating rubberized ablative impact bladder on its underside to cushion the landing shock.

Crewmen would remain inside the B-70's escape capsule during the entire ejection process. North American claimed that safe emergency ejections were possible over a range of from 90 kias on takeoff to Mach 3 at altitudes of about 70,000 feet.

Survival equipment, cold-weather clothing and enough food and water for several days were stored aboard the capsule. If it landed on water the capsule would float like a boat and was equipped with fishing tackle and an inflatable life raft. On January 30, 1960, USAF Airman B. Barwise completed a 72-hour test

62

XB-70A-1 cockpit details. Note large display showing fuel management; XB-70A-2 had display showing location of fuel in its tanks. Pilots considered this to be the best instrument in the cockpit. Rockwell via Boswell

afloat in a survival capsule designed for use in the B-70.

Crew Cabin

Crew duties and equipment design requirements for the B-70 aircraft were analyzed in great detail to determine the most efficient integration of man and machine. The result was ample roominess, foldout control assemblies and color-coded instrument displays correlated to achieve a work environment of maximum efficiency and comfort.

Both XB-70A instrument panels were illuminated with white light to improve visibility over previous red lighting, and indications were given in appropriate directions and positions. Altitude, for example, was shown on a vertical tape scale rather than the circular-type of old style instruments. A combination digital readout and tape-type fuel quantity display gauge was used by B-70 crewmen. The primary flight instrument was the B-70's three-axis display which indicated pitch (the angular displacement about an axis parallel to the lateral axis of the vehicle), roll (the longitudinal axis through an aircraft about which the body rolls), and yaw (the rotational or oscillatory movement of an aircraft about a vertical axis). Axis is a real or imaginary straight line passing through a body that actually or supposedly revolves upon it.

Flight Control System

The XB-70A's flight control system was operated by hydraulic fluid power.

Each of the flight surface control actuators, including wing fold motors, was constructed in a dual-stage arrangement to overcome failure within part of the system. Primary system 1 (P1) was powered by the primary hydraulic pumps on engines 1, 2 and 3. The parallel system P2, was powered by engines 4, 5 and 6. During flight, each of the dual-stage surface actuators was continuously pressurized. The first stage operated at about 3,500 pounds per square inch maximum drop, and the second stage at the average return back-pressure of 500 psi.

The elevons were split into 12 individual segments, each panel operated by a pair of dual actuators to share the load evenly. When each wingtip was folded by its six 32,000-to-1 ratio hinge motors, the two outboard elevons actuators were connected to the pilot's controls by a conventional arrangement of cables and associated tension regulators. The canard surface actuator was linked to the control columns through a series of rods. Provisions were made for the pilot to override the rudders and horizontal canard-type stabilizer by means of complex-geometry cable and rod inputs from override bungees working in parallel to normal inputs. The rudders were not to become effective below 80 to 90 kias during ground roll, and to insure good response at all speeds, they were driven at two different gear ratios (limits were plus or minus 3 degrees with the undercarriage retracted).

To damp out oscillation about all three axes (pitch, roll and yaw), North American's Autonetics Division designed and built a flight augmentation control system (FACS) which consisted of: (1) A sensor package, (2) Four hydraulic servo actuators, consisting of two yaw sensors, a single pitch servo and one roll servo and (3) Two computers.

FACS automatically furnished trim control signals and, in order to keep within structural design loads, it would subtract from inadvertent excessive loads commanded by the pilot. FACS could take over to provide effective flight surface control in the event of mechanical flight control failure. The electronics part of the system was designed fail-safe by means of dual channels in all axes with inter-channel monitoring circuit disengaged that particular section and warned the pilot he must take over in that mode.

Hydraulic Fluid System

The two XB-70A aircraft used more hydraulic equipment and fluid power than any previous plane. Weight limitations ruled out the use of old style hydraulic systems, and because the B-70 cruised at M3 generating extreme temperatures, conventional hydraulic fluids could not be considered. North American saved as much as 10,000 pounds over previous fitting-tubing designs by using brazed fittings and number 350 thin-wall steel tubing. This method of plumbing also helped to insure against leakage within the B-70's vast hydraulic fluid system.

The Vickers Division of Sperry Rand Corporation sub-contracted to provide four independent 4,000 pounds-per-square-inch constant pressure systems pressurized by 12 engine-driven, positive-displacement, variable-output hydraulic pumps for each aircraft. Included within the system were 85 linear actuators, 50 mechanical valves, 44 hydraulic motors and about 400 electrically operated solenoid valves. More than a mile of piping supplied the main services with about 3,300 brazed connections and approximately 600 mechanical joints. Hydraulic fluid capacity within each B-70 totalled 220 U.S. gallons at room temperature and 260 gallons at the maximum operating temperature.

Prior practices in aircraft hydraulics were

During XB-70's flight test program North American investigated jet engine noise pollution, devised this noise abatement device which sent both noise and exhaust skyward. *Rockwell via Boswell*

abandoned by North American in their quest for reliability. Initially, a search for a hydraulic fluid able to withstand the specified minus 65° F to plus 450° F temperature range (plus 275° F is a normal limit) was the order of the day. Of course, a non-flammable fluid was preferred, but none was available. B-70 engineers studied thermal stability, bulk modulus, viscosity, lubricating qualities as well as fluid weights. Due to the fact that the B-70's hydraulic fluid system was purged free of oxygen and sealed, less attention was given to foaming and oxidation issues. At first, both North American and Vickers settled on Oronite 8200 hydraulic fluid but quit it for the newly developed Oronite 70 which had much better overall properties. However, even that particular fluid left much to be desired, since it also failed to meet all criteria. This ultimately led to problems in the designing of the B-70's hydraulic hardware.

Because the B-70's hydraulic fluid reservoirs were pressurized with dry nitrogen, small amounts of that gas dissolved in the fluid and, because Oronite 70 has a high affinity for both air and nitrogen, compressibility problems arose. For example, if the pressure was lowered the nitrogen gas would leave the solution, leaving the fluid aerated, which caused pump cavitation and ultimately leakage within the system. Vickers admitted that their research continued to aim at improving the fluid and that they had initiated an endurance test program with newer variations.

The four basic hydraulic fluid systems provided fluid power to seven of the B-70's subsystems: one, the primary flight-control, vertical stabilizers, elevons, and augmentation; two, the secondary flight-control, wingfold, canard trimmer and flap; three, the landing gear, legs and doors, nose wheel steering and wheel brakes; four, armament mechanism and weapons bay door platforms; five, the environmental drive, compressors, heat-loop pumps, blower fans and floodflow system; six, the utility, emergency generator drive, the drag chute system and windshield ramp; and seven, the propulsion and air induction control systems, and the fuel transfer and boost systems.

The B-70 incorporated two primary (P1 and P2) and two utility (U1 and U2) hydraulic fluid systems, making up the four basic systems mentioned above. Three pumps in a typical master-slave arrangement powered each system. For normal operations, one master pump supplied continuous hydraulic fluid power. Idling until the system demanded increased flow were two salvo pumps which stayed on line, depressurized to about 250 psi for maximum

cooling and lubrication. The slave pumps automatically made themselves available to maintain system pressure at a lower output should a master pump fail.

The pumps were axial-piston, fixed-angle, variable-output-types displacing 5 cubic inches per revolution at 500 revolutions per minute in the P1 and P2 systems, and 2.69 cu in/rev at 6,000 rpms in the U1 and U2 systems. At minimum allowable volumetric efficiency, including compressibility factors, each primary system delivered 276 U.S. gallons per minute and each utility system pumped 180 gpm.

Both primary systems operated as a constant output motor for engine starting. For motor operation, the pump's outlet ports were pressurized through internal valves. During engine start the utility system pumps were depressurized to reduce cranking drag. The B-70 was self-sufficient and could start one engine with a cartridge-type starter and then use that running engine to provide hydraulic starting power to the other five engines; engine starting power was also provided by an external ground power unit. The B-70's hydraulic starting system saved about 380 pounds and notable volume. The external GPU supplied fluid to the engine pump/motor at 60 gpm until the motor reached engine-idling speed (about 5,000 rpms), at which point it received a signal input to convert to pumping. In the event of a control signal malfunction, an automatic shut-off was provided. Early in the design phase of the XB-70A systems, an auxiliary fly-away engine starting pod was considered as a means of making the proposed bomber independent of ground-based external starting power units.

Many of the 36 Vickers-built hydraulic motors were used primarily in fuel system applications. Five of them drove the centrifugal fuel boost pumps; 26 the centrifugal fuel transfer pumps; 4 the wingfold mechanism (not to be confused with the 12 electrically operated power hinges); and 1 pump operated the emergency generator. All of these pumps were fixed-angle, axial-piston, motors which offered either constant or variable torque forces. They ranged in size from 0.097 cubic inch per revolution to 0.62 cu. in./rev. More than 4,000 lb. were saved by designing the pumps without a separate case fluid return system. RPM speed regulation or limiting mechanisms (governors) were built into the pump system. The primary pumps offered a rate-of-flow of 95 gpm and the utility pumps 57 gpm.

The operational oil temperature was about 400° F for the pump inlets and 450° F for the bulk oil and those temperatures were greatly exceeded by compartment temperatures. All the hydraulic actuators and valves had to withstand high heat-soak temperatures to avoid large weight penalties in the cooling of static equipment. The B-70's fuel system made an abundant heat-sink, and was used as such, it approached its predicted 30,000 British Thermal Units (BTUs) per minute limit. This heating problem was eased by using the aforementioned master/slave redundant design combination, which in fact reduced pump heat-rejection by a total of 5,000 BTU/min and by doing so reduced an estimated 1,000 pounds from the entire B-70 cooling system. The remainder of heat was soaked up by the B-70's fuel system.

Each of the system reservoirs featured an integral fuel-to-oil heat exchanger with a temperature-controlled thermal by-pass valve, a temperature-compensated capacitance-type liquid level probe, relief valves and special provisions for operation under sustained negative-G loading. These reservoirs, and most of the hydraulic fluid distribution system, were located within the Valkyrie's integral fuel tanks.

For testing on the ground, provisions were made to test the efficiency of each pump without their removal from the aircraft. Each engine was operated individually, and output for each of the pumps was measured on a ground service unit. Each outlet line contains a 10-micron nominal, 25-micron absolute non-by passing filter. All the aircraft's hydraulic fluid was refiltered through bypass filters in the return system, and in the pump case return lines. No other filters were installed within the system.

North American's analysis of failures due to fluid losses, using their own F-100 Super Sabre fighter plane as an example, showed that more than 60% of these failures could be traced directly to hose fittings and tubing. Two out of three leaks were attributed to either a fitting/tubing combination failure or improper assembly; the remainder lay in the hose of tubing itself. Within the B-70, pressure lines ranged in size to 1.625 inches overall diameter, and return lines to 1.875 in o.d. Besides creating too much weight, conventional fittings would most likely have been as troublesome as their predecessors. North American's attempt to alleviate that particular problem led to the following cures: permanent (brazed) joints wherever possible, tubing with high strength-to-weight ratio at the top of the temperature scale; low-torque threaded fittings, which could be installed without specific torque values; and built in relative motion between components and structure to be taken up by flexible joints and swivels in all-metallic hose, coiled tubing or similar devices.

The B-70 hydraulic lines were manufactured of two types of number 350 cold reduced extrusion steel (CRES) tubing. Cold reduced and tempered (CRT) tubing of 180,000 psi minimum altimate tensile strength was used for all general plumbing; annealed No. 350 CRES, sub-zero-cooled and tempered was used for elbows, tees and other standard fittings. Machined fittings were kept to a minimum; tees and crosses were machine welded, and lines with fittings were brazed with silver-copper-lithium. North American insisted that if previous standard practices had been followed, the B-70's hydraulic system would have weighed at least 10,000 pounds more than it did.

North American realized from the outset that temperature and pressure problems within the hydraulic system would ultimately extend to other system components. Therefore new seals had to be developed as well as new manufacturing processes to cope with new materials. The linear actuators ranged in size from 1-inch diameter up to 7.25 in., and in stroke from several to 30 in. Actuator cylinder barrels were designed to burst pressure only, to save weight. In that way, a large tandem actuator weighing less than 300 lb. could exert a force of more than 300,000 pounds. Some actuators were pressurized continuously, which of course, led to seal failures. B-70 designers admitted that perfecting seal designs was exceptionally difficult, since time-proven elastomer rings had to be tossed out. In their replacement, the constantly pressurized two-stage slight-control actuators were equipped with two-stage dynamic rod seals, while the intermittently pressurized actuators, as used in the landing gear retraction cyclinders, used single stage dynamic rod seals.

Power Plant Systems

Both XB-70A aircraft were powered by six afterburning General Electric YJ93-GE-3 turbojet engines rated in the 30,000 pound static thrust class. The J93 was a single-shaft, axial-flow (the airflow is along the longitudinal axis) turbojet with a variable-stator compressor, fully-variable converging-diverging exhaust nozzle and better than 5-to-1 thrust-to-engine-weight ratio. It was 237 inches long, 52.7 inches deep, and 42 inches across at the face of the air inlet. It burned JP-6 fuel instead of boron chemical fuel, as originally planned for the earlier YJ93-GE-5 model.

Paul L. Dawson, Project Manager for the GE J93, offered his insight as to why the chemical

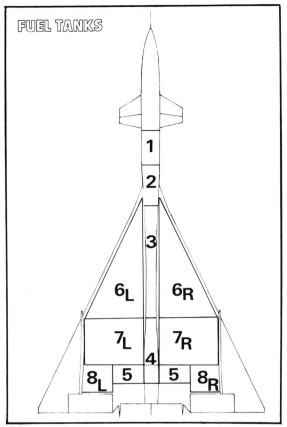

FUEL TANKS

1
2
3
6L 6R
7L 7R
4
8L 5 5 8R

XB-70A fuel tank placement. Fuselage had five tanks; tank 5 leaked in XB-70A-1 and was not used. Each wing had 3 tanks. It was proposed that each wingtip would have a fuel tank, but this plan was dropped. Production B-70s, however, may have had wingtip tanks.   *Author's Collection*

or "zip" fuel-burning YJ93-GE-5 engine was abandoned in favor of the more conventional jet petroleum power plant. "Boron fuel was only considered for application in the after-burner section and some tests were actually run utilizing it. Aside from problems with borate deposits on the afterburner and nozzle parts, the plume of smoke produced would have rendered the application of this fuel impractical, especially on takeoff. It was truly awesome even from one engine and the thought of six of them running this way boggles the imagination. I'm sure it would have created a cloud that would have persisted for days. The environmentalists would have had a field day, even in that time of just awakening concern for the impact on the earth." The boron fuel program was cancelled by the DOD in 1959.

The J93 design was made feasible with several technical breakthroughs combined with already proven design features associated with GE's J79 turbojet engine. GE's Flight Propulsion Division near Cincinnati, Ohio, designed and developed the J93. Six of them pro-

duced about 200,000 horsepower at Mach 3 cruise and proved their worth when they propelled XB-70A-2 to 3 Mach for a sustained flight of 32 minutes on May 19, 1966. Interestingly, the J93 was rated at Mach 4.0!

General Electric put its J93 through rigorous tests, more than 5,000 hours at both sea level and simulated altitudes. Over 700 of these hours were spent at conditions exceeding M2. Final checkout tests were conducted at Edwards AFB prior to B-70 flight testing. This was accomplished with a specially designed engine nacelle, suspended off the underbelly of a modified Convair NB-58A Hustler which replaced its weapon/fuel pod and housed a production-type GE J93-GE-3. The power plant was tested in that unique configuration to investigate air starts, transonic control, afterburning qualities and ground handling characteristics. While in flight with the 30,000-plus pound thrust J93 lit, the Hustler's own four GE J79s had to be throttled back from their normal cruise power settings.

In the XB-70A aircraft, all six J93 engines were interchangeable with a plug-in feature whereby one engine could be removed and replaced in 25 minutes or less. The engine also featured automatic thrust control, eliminating troublesome cables and associated hardware. Accessories and controls were located in a removable pod suspended under the compressor section. The compressor was of moderate pressure ratio and was housed in a split compressor casing for ease of inspection and maintenance, as was the casing over its two-stage turbine which featured air-cooled blades permitting operating temperatures "several hundred degrees higher" than on previous turbojet engines. With the advent of the J93 engine, GE pioneered air-cooled turbines and the use of titanium alloy turbine blades. The latter became nicked and scratched more frequently than conventional steel blades in other engine applications, however, and the engines demonstrated their sensitivity to ingestion of foreign objects. Throughout phase 1 flight testing, twenty-five J93s were replaced due to inflight ingestion of foreign materials; five changes due to damage incurred on the ground. To eliminate ground damage, custom-built screens were fitted to the B-70's two air inlets for run-ups. This way objects could not accumulate within the craft's inlet tunnels to be sucked into the vulnerable engines later.

In an effort to alleviate the engine noise problem North American ran a series of noise abatement tests. Ultimately, NAA designers designed a device which not only quieted the J93 engines during a static run-ups, but, distributed their heat and smoke upwards away from mechanics working in the immediate vicinity of the craft. It was GE's basic J93 engine design which eventually led to their creation of the awesome 50,000 pound thrust Model GE-4.

GE built 38 J93 engines before the B-70 program was terminated. With a combined thrust rating of over 185,000 pounds, North American claimed that even with one engine out the B-70 would still maintain M3 cruise with only a 7 per cent loss in range. The J93 was the first turbojet engine designed for operation in continuous afterburner. In fact, the J93 operated more efficiently at speeds exceeding Mach 2.7. Design limit for the XB-70A was M3, however, airframe design and materials could have extended the limit to Mach 4 according to North American, but major revision in its environmental control and hydraulic fluid systems would have been required.

Fuel System

Each B-70 incorporated eleven separate integral fuel tanks which held approximately 47,000 U.S. gallons of JP-6 fuel weighing nearly 300,000 pounds or about two-thirds of the B-70's total gross weight. JP-6 is a highly refined JP-4 (the type commonly used by commercial airliners with improved heat stability and resistance to the formation of solids. Port wing tanks were numbered 6, 7 and 8 left; starboard wing tanks 6, 7 and 8 right; fuselage tanks were numbered 1, 2, 3, 4 and 5 fore-to-aft. The rearmost fuselage tank on XB-70A No. 1 became increasingly difficult to seal and therefore was never used. However, that U-shaped number 5 tank was utilized on XB-70A-2, as it was the beneficiary of improved manufacturing techniques and a later discovered sealant called Viton-B. Thus, fuel capacity of the second ship increased.

Brazed stainless steel honeycomb sandwich panel construction insulated the fuel system and protected it from aerodynamic heating. The maximum operating temperature was 260°F and thus was used as a heat-sink by the hydraulic, engine oil and compartment-cooling systems. At 2,000 mph cruise speeds the system's heat-rejection rate reached about 30,000 BTUs/min. Fuel tank number 3 was located over the aircraft's center of gravity, therefore it was selected to be utilized as a sump for all fuel flowing to the engines at a cruise-speed rate of 785 pounds per minute at 300°F. Fuel was programmed into tank No. 3 by an automatic system. Each fuel tank had two transfer pumps controlled by two fuel-level valves in tank number 3, which drained the remaining tanks in sequence for best trim.

The pilot could monitor the entire system during auto-sequence with fuel-gauging working on capacitance. If a malfunction presented itself in the sequencing devices, the system could be operated manually and contents of each tank noted individually. Manual fuel management, however, would be difficult during climb out, when an estimated 30% of the total fuel load might be expended. Common lines were used for both transfer and refueling. Hydraulic fluid power drove all transfer and booster pumps in the fuel system (refer to **Hydraulic System**).

Designing the B-70 fuel system to act as a heat-sink for cooling the "hot" systems required that consideration be given to the points at which the fuel quantity was low or when fuel flows were reduced when the engines were throttled back. The system was made flexible, and more complicated, by the addition of 400 lb. of water to act as a substitute heat-sink. The water was vaporized at the rate of 28 lb./min. in a boiler by heat-transfer from the engine-oil, hydraulic and environmental control cooling systems. Consequently the water's latent heat of vaporization extracted excess heat at the points where or when the fuel could not, thus keeping all systems below their maximum operating temperatures. In the fuel coolant-loop, fuel in excess of engine demands returned to the tank after passing through the heat exhangers.

As B-70 fuel tank quantity went down, the ever increasing temperature of the fuel could create an explosive mixture. As the presence of oxygen in the tanks was thought to contribute to fuel degradation, both conditions were avoided by sealing the tanks and by pumping in a nitrogen gas blanket over the fuel at 9 pounds per square inch. Weight consideration precluded carrying a large capacity liquid nitrogen gas storage system to top off tank pressure as its fuel was used. Gas leakage from the tanks had to be kept at an absolute minimum, since lost dry nitrogen would be replaced by air. It was for this reason that the minute pinholes, discovered when the main sections of the No. 1 B-70 were welded together, had to be completely sealed.

B-70 design criteria for the fuel system specified that all tanks had to be pressurized to 10 psi with zero leakage, as construction progressed, the manufacturing and design groups thought they were holding to all requirements. But engineering changes, weld stresses and areas where it was not considered important to test-pressurize, combined to create an accumulation of leakage problems. Brazing repairs to the leaking areas proved ineffective. A non-metallic material made by DuPont called Viton-

B was eventually used to coat the porous areas. A single coat of Viton was painted on, and then cured for six hours while heated to 375°F by electric blankets (even hair dryers in some inaccessible areas). The application process was repeated six times before sealing was considered to be complete. Helium was then used to pressurize the tanks, and "sniffers" detected remaining leaks. The time consumed in arriving at this cure, and difficulty of application (on the average, ten tries per tank) amounted to many months. Even at that, North American's materials engineers specified that the Viton-B would have to be stripped from XB-70A-1 after 1,000 hours and have its tanks resealed, but that particular problem never materialized, as B-70 No. 1 accumulated only 160:18 total hours of flight time.

Fueling the B-70 was an elaborate procedure requiring up to 1½ hours. That fact would have possibly presented SAC with a time problem, as they have almost habitually boasted about response time. Initially, a tanker starts pumping its fuel into a second empty tanker standing nearby. Meanwhile a second tanker is pressurized by high-pressure dry nitrogen which is bubbled through JP-6 entering its inlet port. The nitrogen gas drives out any oxygen present within the jet petroleum fuel, so that the JP-6 pumped into the aircraft is already pressurized with nitrogen and as inert as it can be possibly made in the field.

For inflight refueling, the B-70 was equipped with a refueling receptacle located ahead of its two-position windshield ramp on centerline. Standard flying book hookups could have been used for mid-air fuel transfer, however, no B-70 inflight refueling data is available.

Electrical System

The B-70 used an all alternating-current electrical power system. The decision by North American to use a 115V to 200V, 400c/s bus system powered by two 240/416 volt primary generators came after studies indicated that considerable weight could be saved by abandoning conventional direct current power. (A bus is an uninsulated conductor—a bar, strip, or wire—used to carry heavy currents or to make a common connection between several points.) As has been realized for some time, 400 cycles per second a.c. devices weigh considerably less than their d.c. counterparts. Power transmission at full generator voltage also proved considerably lighter, although transformers located near the load centers were required to step generator voltage down to bus level.

The B-70's electrical power system was con-

ventional in layout. It consisted of three main junctions: left, right and essential. Power for the essential bus was provided on an as needed basis by a 120/208 volt emergency generator driven by a hydraulic fluid power motor. The 60kVA primary generators, weighing 1.6 lb/kW, were of the brushless rotating rectifier type, eliminating arcing even at extreme altitudes.

The B-70's generator therefore delivered twice normal voltage (440V), permitting huge savings in the weight of the main feeder cable used for power transmission.

The high voltage a.c. distribution system was an improvement over the a.c. and low voltage d.c. combination systems used on previous aircraft, which required multiple wiring. The B-70's system was made possible by technical breakthroughs in design of high temperature components such as lightweight wire connectors, switches, a.c. relays and motors.

The two 40kVA 240/416V alternators were located on the number 3 and 4 engines. The six 60kVA a.c. generators weighed 300 lb. each. They operated successfully at temperatures of about 550°F, transmitting 440 volts through 140 feet of three-wire feeder cable to lightweight transformers at the bus network located in the forward, controlled environment electronics bay.

Landing Gear and Braking Systems

A rugged landing gear weighing more than six tons and consisting of two tons of wheels, tires, and brakes supported the B-70 aircraft on the ground. Each main gear had four wheels and the nose gear had two wheels. The high temperatures to which the gear was subjected required tires capable of operation at 360°F. Hydraulic actuators for the gear utilized metal seals to permit operation up to about 600°F.

The landing gear for the B-70 had several distinguishing features. Each main gear was made up of a bogey with a brake stack of 21 stationary and 20 revolving discs located between the paired wheels and tires at each end. The stationary discs were splined onto a stator ring cage, and the rotating discs were splined to the torque tube to which the wheels were attached. The wheels rotated on bearings fitted directly to the H-11 forged steel bogey instead of an axle. By separating the brake discs from the wheels, more efficient cooling was achieved.

In a single stop, the B-70's braking system had to absorb kinetic energy equal to that used in stopping 800 mid-sized automobiles from a speed of about 100 mph. Moreover, they had to withstand temperatures approaching 1,800°F.

A conventional system would most likely blow the tires at the 2,000°F brake temperatures generated by the maximum stopping requirement, where nearly 200 million foot pounds of kinetic energy were absorbed. In tests simulating deceleration with brake stress 20% over design requirements, the brakes took 45 seconds, or 6,500 feet of runway to reach zero acceleration. Tire temperatures in these tests reached 250°F, almost 200° under the 460°F relief-valve setting of deflation.

To provide protection against skidding and blowouts, a unique brake control device employing a "fifth wheel" was designed into the B-70's braking system. Designed to allow maximum braking without skidding, the device compared to amount of slippage between the braked wheels and the fifth wheel with the coefficient of friction between the tires and the runway surface—then predicted the exact point at which the tires would go into a skid. The brakes were then automatically regulated to prevent skidding. In this system a small 16x-4.4 inch type VII fifth wheel measured the true ground speed of the aircraft with no slippage, and transmitted the information to the onboard brake system computer. One of the main gear wheels also contained a speed sensor which in turn transmitted its speed to the computer. One of the main gear wheels also contained a speed sensor which in turn transmitted its speed to the computer. The difference between the two outputs was the amount of slippage taking place. Measurement of the amount of load on the wheels transmitted to the computer by a torque sensor enabled the computer to determine the ground speed coefficient. Above 15% slippage a comparison between the rate of slippage and the ground coefficient predicted the skid point, and the brake pressure to that particular wheel was automatically relieved. Another way to explain the foregoing is to use an example of Gracie Allen's method of cooking. She would always buy two roasts, one large and one small, and would put both in the oven at the same time. When the small roast burned, the big one was ready to serve.

The B.F. Goodrich Company claimed that conventional aircraft tires would not withstand the B-70's inflight wheel well compartment heat, let alone the landing and braking temperatures. Improvements in the materials used in the 40x17½-18 type VIII tires allowed a load-carrying capacity double that of conventional tires of equal weight. The 36-ply rating tires and their wheels were the same all around.

Silver coloring of the tires was due to a heat resistant material painted on the exterior surface as well as being impregnated throughout

the body of the tire. Tires were not repainted during normal operations, but prior to a mission of long duration they were retouched with the reflective material and, their surfaces were cleaned. The 4-ply rate fifth wheel was not silver colored; it was made of dark heat-resistant material which did not require heat re-

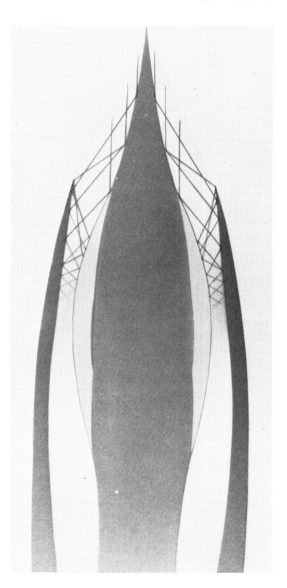

For the XB-70A's six J93 engines to operate effectively, air entering them had to be slowed to less than Mach 1. To do this, North American developed an Air Induction control System (AICS). This AICS, working by variable-geometry, adjusted the size of B-70's inlet throats; air entering B-70's ducts was effectively slowed to MO.5. Illustration shows airflows slowing before entering B-70's 7-foot high, 80-foot long inlet ducts. XB-70A-2 featured a computerized AICS, whereas XB-70A-1's was manual. XB-70A-1 was retrofit later with a computerized AICS, however.
Rockwell

XB-70A-1 being prepared for its 83rd and final flight to Wright-Patterson AFB, Ohio, on February 4, 1969, where it was presented to the Air Force Museum. Note exiter or shaker vanes on nose ahead of canards, down flaps on canard foreplanes, down elevon on wings and instrument boom. Also note boundary layer air bleed-off slots above intake throats. Rockwell

flection to withstand high temperatures. The wheel walls of the B-70 were held to a nominal 250°F by circulating an ethelene-glycol solution from the environmental control system through tubing brazed to the walls.

The B-70's nose wheel steering control also incorporated a new concept with complete fail-safe provisions. Previous systems were capable of detecting emergencies only after they occurred, but the B-70's system detected a malfunction, they compensated for it automatically before conditions became serious.

Air Induction Control System

The two XB-70As featured a variable-geometry air induction control system (AICS). One of the most critical problems associated with supersonic aircraft design is keeping the air-breathing turbojet engines properly supplied with air. Air must be fed to them at the correct rate-of-flow, and with uniformly high pressure. Air blasted into the inlet at M3 speeds must be efficiently slowed and delivered to the face of the engines at subsonic speeds; Mach 0.50 is preferred.

The B-70's AICS began with a rectangular, twin 65x47 inch variable throat air inlet with boundary layer bleed. About 90% of the air compression was performed within the twin intake tunnels, which were about 80 feet long and 7 feet high at the duct end. Temperature of the air was raised to a maximum of 630°F during aerodynamic compression. This created an approximate ratio of 36-to-1 prior to entry into the six GE J93 engines. The inlet was designed to reduce the free-stream air velocity from plus or minus Mach 3 to less than Mach 1 by a series of shocks, beginning with the primary shock wave created by the leading edge of the vertical splitter duct and ending aft of the minimum throat area. But such factors as gust disturbances—which would cause the shock to "pop out" of the duct—would result in engine unstart, and required that it be positioned farther back as a safety margin.

Introducing the initial shock into the inlet was called "starting" the inlet. If a situation arose where the shock came out of the inlet, it was called an "unstart." An unstart was not a dangerous phenomenon, though it occurred with a severe jolt and could cause a loss of thrust. It could lead to "duct buzz" which developed when the shock came out of the inlet, went back in and came out in an oscillating manner. Duct buzz created tremendous pressure fluctuations within the inlet and was considered the most critical condition the inlet structure might encounter in flight.

Two secondary shocks prior to the duct entrance were caused by breaks in the sweep angle of the splitter duct. The air followed a circular route in the duct, which caused another series of shocks. The terminal shock to subsonic velocity was last to occur. Three movable panels, positioned by two hydraulic actuators, opened and closed the throat area to meet engine air rate-of-flow requirements. Position of the shock was controlled by opening or closing a series of bypass doors on the upper surface of the wing. The three panels in the throat were perforated so that slow moving turbulent boundary layer air was bled to ambient pressure on the other side of the panels. This provided better distribution of the inlet air across the face of the engines.

A three-position switch in the cockpit allowed the pilot to choose how far forward or aft the terminal shock would be positioned. For maximum range and most efficient air recovery, the shock was positioned forward. Depending on flight conditions/requirements, amount of maneuvering and turbulence, it would be positioned at the intermediate or aft locations. The aft location provided the most stable operation and precluded the chance of the shock being expelled through the front of the duct.

Initially, XB-70A No. 1 was outfitted with a manually operated AICS, whereas XB-70A No. 2 benefited from a fully automatic computerized air induction control system. Ship No. 1's manual AICS was replaced with an automatic system later in the flight test program.

Computations required to achieve proper inlet/duct operation under the always changing flight conditions were performed by a complex system of probes which fed information to onboard computers, which in turn generated signals instructing the refined electro-mechanical system to assume optimum throat and bypass positions. This system was housed in the 30-foot long bomb bay and weighed 4,400 pounds.

Weapons System

Both XB-70A prototypes were constructed with functional bomb bays (referred to as weapons bay today) about 30 feet long and featured North American engineered flat translating doors for the ease of high supersonic speed weapons delivery. The B-70's weapons bay was designed to house about 25 tons of varied free falling nuclear-type or conventional iron bombs. But its weapons bay provided a haven for various test equipment instead.

At one point in the B-70's development, consideration was given to incorporation of wing-mounted hard-points for pylon stations for either the Hound Dog or Skybolt air-launched missiles. Also under consideration was an onboard self-defense missile system to eliminate requirement for fighter escort support. One problem associated with the inflight launching of missiles at the speeds of which the B-70 was capable is separation. Mission requirements clearly specified that the B-70 bomber be at high-Mach speeds during weapons delivery; to effectively launch a ballistic missile from an air-

B-52H Stratofortress carrying four dummy Douglas GAM-87 Skybolt two-stage, solid-propellant air-to-surface ballistic missiles. As proposed, production B-70s would have been armed similarly. Boeing via Brooks

73

craft during flight, slower subsonic speeds are preferred. To slow the B-70 during its attack run upon a target would completely defeat the purpose for which it was intended. As it ulti- mately turned out, high-altitude, high-speed weapons delivery is no longer practical for an attacking bomber plane; low-altitude, high-subsonic speed weapons delivery is.

Convair's WS-125A proposal which called for two nuclear engines in the tail and two conventional engines mounted under wings. Convair model number was NX-2 for this particular version of the nuclear-powered bomber (NPB). A 1945 von Karman report saw this type of airplane in the distant future. He said, "the problem should be attacked urgently."   *General Dynamics*

Chapter Four
Flight Testing & Retirement

North American's hypersonic X-15A-2 rocket plane posing along side triplesonic XB-70A-1 at Edward AFB. Both aircraft gathered millions of bits of aerodynamic data to benefit mankind for years to come.   NASA

Dotted with buildings, like cardboard cutouts, dwarfed by the vastness of area, the Air Force Flight Test Center at Edwards Air Force Base, California, is a sprawling mass of concrete and dry lakebed on a high desert plain, a part of the Mojave Desert. Tumbleweeds peer in through cyclone fences, crowding for the best view. Isolated from the densely populated coast by desert and mountain. Edwards has been the proving grounds for many a new airplane. It also was for the XB-70 Valkyrie.

Flight Testing

The road to Edwards was a rocky and perilous path for the B-70. Originally intended to fly in 1961, then 1962, then 1963, the B-70 finally took wing in 1964, ten years after its inception.

At 8:38 a.m., on September 21, 1964, XB-70A number one rotated at 183 knots indicated airspeed at Palmdale's 5,000-foot marker and climbed up and away to begin its flight test program. To enable North American to collect a $250 thousand bonus, the flight plan called for a 1-hour, 45-minute flight test to culminate with a Mach 1 dash at 35,000 feet.

At the helm were North American's chief engineering test pilot Alvin S. (Al) White and USAF project pilot Colonel Joseph F. Cotton. Following rotation, canard flaps and landing gear retracted. However, the main gear refused command, the nose gear was re-extended. It was decided to proceed on a pre-planned, secondary low speed flight test plan. Then while flying at 255 KIAS at 16,000 feet, number 3 engine tachometer showed an overspeed of 108% rpm. Pilot White immediately shut down that engine. Following a 1-hour, 7-minute flight on five engines, White landed XB-70A-1 at Edwards AFB on runway 04. But, not without further difficulty. As the heavy prototype (landing weight was 307,340 pounds) rolled out its momentum, trailing its three 28-foot diameter drag chutes behind, the rear two wheels on the left main bogie refused to rotate, tires blew, sparks and fire trailed behind. B-70 had touched down at 181 KIAS by the 2,000-foot marker and it came to a stop just past the 13,000-foot marker, using 10,800 feet to stop. During rollout the pilots didn't notice the drag of the blown tires and no directional control problems were encountered. The aircraft remained on the runway until about 6 p.m., undergoing on the spot repairs. New bogie, wheels and tires were installed after the craft had been

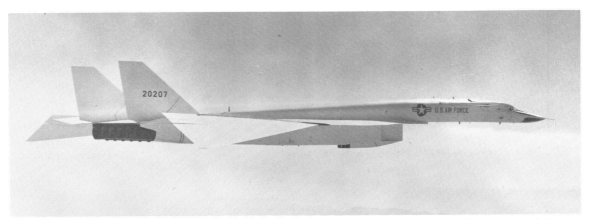

XB-70A-2 during first flight test. Wingtips are in mid-down configuration. Note that fuselage appears to be an airfoil itself, generating vortex off its top.   *Rockwell*

XB-70A-1 heads skyward on its maiden flight from USAF Plant 42, Palmdale, California. Flight lasted 1 hour 7 minutes and ended at Edwards AFB.   *Rockwell*

XB-70A-1 moments into the first flight; rotation occurred at 4,853 feet and 181 kias. Flight began at 8:38 a.m. 21 September 1964, ended at 9:45 a.m. Al White (pilot) and Joe Cotton (copilot) reported that the aircraft flew very well. Note heat waves generated by six GE J93 engines.   *Rockwell*

defueled. It was then towed into a hangar. Regardless of these mishaps, both White and Cotton reported that the plane had flown well. North American did not collect the quarter million dollar bonus.

Flight test No. 2 occurred two weeks later on October 5, again at the hands of White and Cotton. Maximum speed and altitude attained during this 55-minute flight was 350 KIAS at 28,000 feet. During this flutter and power control flight test, the No. 1 utility hydraulic system leaked, the landing gear had to be extended under emergency conditions using the B-70's electrical backup system, and the aircraft had to make an emergency landing on the lakebed, during which, one of the drag chutes refused to deploy.

If Mach 1 had been attained during flight test No. 2, NAA was to receive a $125 thousand bonus. But the flight was terminated early and only Mach 0.85 was reached. Thus under contract penalty, NAA had to pay $125,000, and the USAF collected it.

White and Cotton performed flight test No. 3 on October 12, it lasted 1-hour, 35-minutes. Mach 1 was attained and White held M 1.11 at 35,400 feet for 15 minutes. During this particular flight test, stability and control, flutter, power control and flight augmentation control system (FACS) tests were performed. The land-

ing gear was recycled immediately after initial cleanup to check on the U-1 hydraulic system. The flight went well but a drag chute opened late during landing rollout.

The fourth flight test, which ended Phase One, came on 24 October. White and Cotton were again at the helm and the flight lasted 1-hour, 25-minutes; Mach 1.42 at 46,300 feet was accomplished. After stability and control, flutter and ram purge tests were performed, whereby the cockpit didn't repressurize, B-70's variable-geometry wingtips were lowered to their mid-down 25 degree position. White landed at Palmdale as XB-70A-1 had to undergo structural stress testing for about four months.

Stress testing completed satisfactorily, Phase Two began on February 16, 1965, when Al White and Joe Cotton took XB-70A-1 up again on flight test number 5. During this flight its wingtips were lowered to their full-down 65 degree deflection, and B-70's manual air inlet control system (AICS) throat ramps were cycled. This flight test lasted 1-hour and 10-minutes, and M 1.6 at 45,000 feet was attained.

Flight testing of XB-70A-1 moved along steadily while it waited for XB-70A-2 to join her. Mach 2.14 at 56,100 feet was reached during flight test 8; Mach 2.6 at 65,000 feet was at-

XB-70A-1 shown just before touchdown following initial flight test on 21 September 1964. Aircraft is about to land on the main runway (17) at Edwards AFB.   *Rockwell*

XB-70As featured three 28-foot diameter braking parachutes housed in a compartment atop fuselage be-tween vertical tails. Here XB-70A-1 nears 8,000 foot marker on an Edwards AFB runway, chutes are fully deployed. *Rockwell via Bear*

Pilot Al White and copilot Joe Cot-ton and others assessing damage to left main landing gear assembly after XB-70A-1's first flight. Bogey wheels and tires had to be re-placed on the spot. *Rockwell*

XB-70A-1 after initial landing at Edwards following first flight test. Personnel under aircraft are surveying damage to left main landing gear as brakes locked during rollout, two tires blew before aircraft stopped. Air-craft used 10,800 feet to stop. *Rockwell via Emmons*

On 24 October 1964, XB-70A-1 was returned to Palmdale where it underwent static structural proof-loading tests until February 1965. Flight testing resumed on 16 February, beginning Phase II.
Rockwell

XB-70A-1 during 5th flight test on 16 February 1965. This particular flight lasted 1 hour 10 minutes; Mach 1.6 at 45,000 feet was attained. It was the first time that A/V-1's wingtips were lowered to full-down. Rockwell

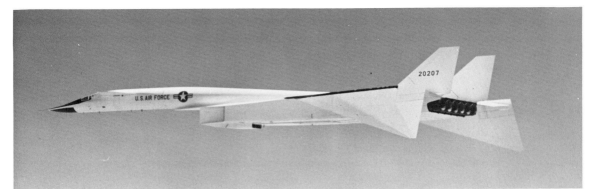

XB-70A-2 during 17th flight test 3 January 1966, where it achieved M3 for the first time; M3.05 at 72,000 feet. Ironically, XB-70A-1 hit M3 on its 17th flight as well. *Rockwell*

On October 14, 1965, XB-70A-1 first hit M3 (M3.02 at 70,000 feet). Al White and Joe Cotton performed this 17th flight test which lasted 1 hour, 47 minutes. On 3 January 1966, these two pilots went M3 again, but in XB-70A-2 on its 17th flight. The planes worked. *Rockwell via Boswell*

tained during flight test 12; and Mach 2.85 at 68,000 feet was accomplished on flight test 14.

Then on July 17,1965, XB-70A number two joined the B-70 flight test program, during which it flew to M 1.41 at 42,000 feet. By its eighth flight test it had attained a speed of M 2.34 at 57,500 feet.

Early flight testing was designed to test all B-70 systems in action. Later, B-70s were equipped with sensitive testing apparatus (over one thousand sensors) to record vital information to be applied in the development of future supersonic aircraft.

Normal climb schedule for B-70 aircraft consisted of a series of accelerations, combined with variations in wingtip, windshield, and air inlet geometry. Gear and flaps were retracted early. Wingtips were lowered to mid-down anywhere from 400 KIAS to 630 KIAS (M 0.95). Steady acceleration followed to 32,000 feet, to 1.5 Mach. At this point, wingtips were lowered to full-down. Mach 1.5 was maintained to about 50,000 feet, then varying rates of acceleration were applied until M3 (2,000 mph) velocity at 70,000 feet were established. Then M3 cruise were maintained. The best recorded time to M3 was 25 minutes from rotation.

From M2 on, B-70's rectangular air inlet ramps began to close. As speed increased, their geometric configuration adjusted for optimum pressure recovery through a series of sequential shocks; beginning with an oblique shock from the splitter plate, ending with a terminal shock as the air reached the throat areas. Ramp movements in the inlets were scheduled by local Mach number due to aircraft yaw, or turbulence, which could cause local variations in air flow. Introducing the initial shock wave was "starting" the inlet ramps.

If the shock wave refused to enter, or popped back out of the inlets, you had an "unstart" condition.

Al White described an unstart at M3 as sudden and violent, accompanied by a large reduction in engine thrust. The aircraft rolled, pitched and yawed, and considerable buffeting was experienced. Normally one inlet unstarted with a bang and after the pilot recovered from that shock, the other inlet would usually unstart.

While not particularly dangerous, unstarting was one problem facing supersonic transport designers. Passengers aboard an SST would not appreciate such an occurrence in flight. Nor would their stomachs.

One flight problem in particular disturbed B-70 pilots. At 2,000 mph, altitude varied some 600 feet. In fact, two or three thousand foot variances were noted. To eliminate this problem, pilots suggested that computerized instrumentation be employed.

On October 14, 1965, during flight test 17, XB-70A number one achieved M3.02 (2,000 mph) at 70,000 feet. Then on January 3, 1966, XB-70A number two reached M3.05 at 72,000 feet. Ironically, both aircraft had reached their M3 goal on flight test 17. On May 19, 1966, XB-70A-2 held M3-plus for 32 full minutes while covering eight states.

While essentially identical to XB-70A-1, certain improvements were made to XB-70A-2. These were: an automated, computerized AICS was installed; a 5 degree dihedral (upwards slant) of the wings was incorporated; a larger fuel capacity (the aft fuel tank in the fuselage) was incorporated; and, additional instrumentation for recording data pertaining to America's SST program was installed.

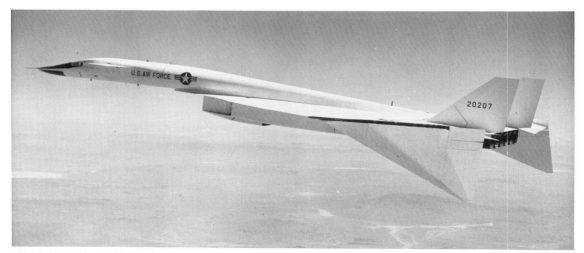

XB-70A-2 during initial flight test 17 July 1965. Mach 1.41 at 42,000 feet was attained during this 1 hour 13 minute flight; 21 minutes spent above Mach 1.0. Note that wingtips are full-down. Rockwell

Crash

B-70 number 2, profited from number 1's mistakes. Internally and externally it was a better ship than its predecessor. The older B-70 had suffered from a malady of complications such as internal hydraulic fluid and fuel leaks and external skin failures during flight. Consequently, XB-70A-1 was reduced to a M2.5 machine while XB-70A-2 was allowed to fly at M3-plus. Just as everything appeared to be going well for ship number two, tragedy struck it down.

It was on June 8, 1966, flight test 2-46, which translates to air vehicle 2, flight test 46, that the tragedy struck. It was the 95th flight test of an XB-70. Al White was in the B-70's pilot seat for his 49th time. In the copilot's seat was a newcomer, USAF Major Carl S. Cross. Cross, a forty-year-old Tennessean, was the seventh man assigned to participate in the B-70 flight test program.

At 7:15 a.m. sharp, XB-70A-2 rotated at 205 KIAS and left behind Edwards' runway 04 after an 8,000-foot takeoff roll. Predetermined flight test objectives consisted of twelve subsonic airspeed calibration runs and a single supersonic boom test run, after which, White and Cross were to rendezvous with a contingent of jet aircraft, all powered by GE engines, for a public relations photographic session. The General Electric Company had obtained USAF approval from B-70 Flight Test Operations a week earlier, permission had been granted to organize a formation of GE-powered aircraft around XB-70A-2 on a non-interference basis.

Participating in this GE-sponsored public relations photo session were: a Northrop F-5A Freedom Fighter flown by GE's test pilot John M. Fritz, who had organized the event; a Northrop T-38 Talon piloted by USAF Captain Peter C. Hoag, with B-70 test pilot USAF Colonel

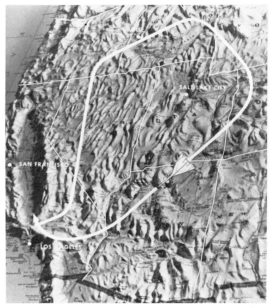

Flight route taken by XB-70-A on May 19, 1966, when it flew at M3 for a period of 32 minutes straight. This was its 39th flight, eight different states were covered. Top speed recorded was M3.06 at 72,500 feet during flight; flight lasted 1 hour 59 minutes.
Rockwell via Boswell

XB-70A-2 during low-level high-speed pass over Edwards accompanied by a Lockheed F-104 Starfighter. Ironically, it was an F-104 that was destined to end its career June 8, 1966, when a NASA F-104 collided with it over the Mojave Desert. That particular tragedy has been called "the blackest day in Edwards' history."
Rockwell

Joseph F. Cotton in its rear seat; a McDonnell F-4B Phantom II flown by USN Commander Jerome P. Skyrud, with E. J. Black in the back; and a NASA F-104N (No. 813) chase aircraft flown by NASA's Joseph A. Walker, chief research pilot. A Gates Lear Jet (likewise GE-powered) flown by H. Clay Lacey, loaded with photographers, recorded the event. Another Starfighter, a two-seat F-104D, piloted by USAF Colonel Sorlie, with an official Air Force photographer aboard, offered photographic back up assistance but wasn't in the immediate area.

Primary flight test duties over, it was time to do some PR work for GE. White descended XB-70A-2 to a lower altitude and raised his wingtips from their full-down to mid-down configuration.

Rendezvous began at 8:27 a.m. when Fritz's F-5 joined XB-70A-2 on a southwesterly heading away from Edwards at 20,000 feet. By 8:43 the rest of the GE-powered aircraft had formed on the B-70 in a V-formation. The B-70 was leading the flock; Walker's F-104N was off its starboard wing; Fritz's F-5 was outboard and to the rear of Walker; Skyrud's F-4 was off its port wing; Hoag's T-38 was outboard and to the rear of Skyrud. The GE-leased Lear Jet was positioned about 200-yards out and to the left of the formation.

The airborne stage was set, it was time to roll cameras.

For a good backdrop, White raised the B-70 to 25,000 feet where he found blue sky. His airspeed indicator read 300 KIAS. Cameras began clicking at 8:45. The photo-taking session was over at 9:25. Suddenly, at 9:26 a.m., aircraft radios crackled frantically. "Mid-air! . . .

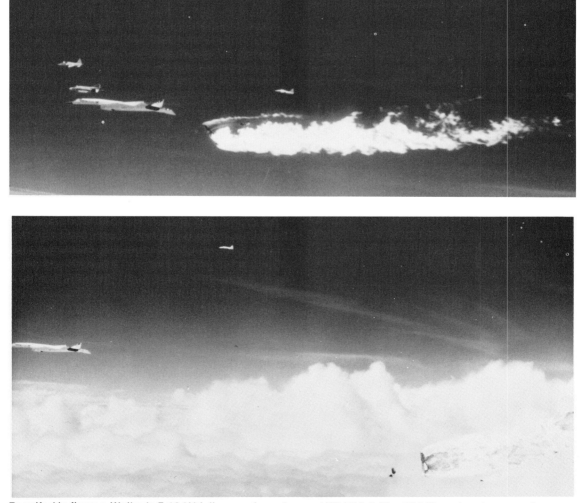

Engulfed in flames, Walker's F-104N falls away from doomed XB-70A-2. The 104 flipped end-over-end, over-and-over while falling to the desert floor some 25,000 feet below. Meanwhile, pilot Al White and copilot Carl Cross wondered what the hell had happened, to whom. USAF via Murone

Without sufficient vertical tail area left to hold XB-70A-2 straight and level, it rolled over on its back nose down, then went into a violent yaw. It was at this moment that White and Cross realized that their craft was doomed. B-70 entered into a flat spin, hit desert in a relatively flat configuration and burned.

USAF via Murone

Mid-air! . . . Mid-air!" Somehow Walker's Starfighter had rammed the B-70. The F-104N's T-tail had hit, ripped at the Valkyrie's drooped right wingtip and his errant craft rolled sharply left, out of control. It then flipped upside down and passed over the B-70's back inverted, shearing off part of its right and most of its left vertical fins. While it was still inverted, the Starfighter pounded away at the Valkyrie's left wing like a crazed woodpecker. Walker was killed instantly. The F-104N burst into flames, ripped into pieces and fell aft and away from the stricken B-70. It twisted violently, flipped over and over through the air in a huge fireball, then fell to the desert floor below. It was all over in about three seconds for the fighter plane. But, it had just begun for the B-70.

As if nothing had occurred, XB-70A-2 flew on, wings straight and level for some 16 seconds. There was no indication in the cockpit that the craft had been mortally wounded—just a distant thump—detached, yet terrifying. Al White turned to Carl Cross and said, "I wonder who it is." Even after they heard the frantic radio calls, neither White nor Cross tied the emergency to their craft. They still did not realize it was their aircraft even when Cotton called, "Your tails are gone; You'll probably spin." Neither B-70 pilot heard the "s" on tail and therefore didn't associate the mid-air collision with their B-70. If they had heard "tails" instead of "tail" they would have known for a fact that it was indeed their craft and that they were in trouble, as it was the only plane in the formation with two tails. XB-70A-2 shuddered, then rolled over on its back, nose down, and went into a violent yaw due to the fact that it no longer had sufficient vertical stabilizer area to hold it straight and level. It was at this point that both pilots knew their ship was doomed.

The airstream hitting XB-70A-2 from such an uncommon angle flipped it through a giant snap roll; fuel spewed from the torn right wing. Both pilots were equipped with individual escape modules. White pulled the ring to encapsulate himself, but for some unknown reason Cross did not. White said later that Cross had not performed the initial step to free himself from the falling craft. It was speculated later that he may have suffered a blow to the head, or that g-forces were too great for him to act. Spinning nose down, the B-70 plummeted to the Mojave Desert floor, some 4 miles N-NE of Barstow, where it impacted in a relatively flat configuration and burned. Walker's F-104N hit earlier some five miles from the B-70, and White's escape pod landed about ten miles north of the B-70 crash site.

Although White had apparently parachuted down through the center of the B-70's spin circle he never saw the plane again. In shock from pain (he had caught his arm in the closing capsule's shell and wrenched his arm out of its shoulder socket as he dragged it inside) and fear, he still knew, somehow, that the air bag designed to cushion the capsule's landing shock had malfunctioned during his frantic fight to free his jammed arm. But, he couldn't remember the secondary sequence for inflating the air bag and, without it, the heavy escape capsule slammed hard into the desert floor with an estimated force of 43 g's. The capsule hit so hard, in fact, that his heels drove deep dents into the metal flooring and his body tore away the entire seating structure. The collapse of the seating structure eased the landing force on White, however, and probably prevented fatal injury, although his internal organs were badly wrenched, causing damage that threatened his life during the next several days.

White guessed that he ejected about a minute after the B-70 went berserk and only a few seconds before it would have been too late. He wasn't rescued until 45 minutes after impact. He didn't learn of his copilot's or Walker's deaths until the next day while he was in recovery at the Edwards AFB hospital, when a visiting priest mentioned to him that he had already talked to the wives of his friends.

Carl Cross was an 8,500-hour veteran of Korea and Vietnam, and had six years of testing in multi-engined jet aircraft. He was making his indoctrination flight in XB-70A-2, and was to replace Fitz Fulton on the B-70's pilot roster.

Joe Walker, 45, had over 5,000 hours of flying time to his credit, he was famous for the altitude and speed marks he had established piloting X-15 rocket planes (354,200 feet,

XB-70A-2 burning after impact some 4 miles N-NE of Barstow, California. Joe Walker's F-104 impacted about 5 miles away and Al White's escape capsule hit about 10 miles north of XB-70A-2's crash site. USAF

4,104 mph). He had flown chase in NASA F-104s eight times before and, ironically, he was to become NASA's chief B-70 test pilot. In fact, his indoctrination flight was to occur two days later, in XB-70A-2.

White and Cross had been assigned to fly XB-70A-2 in the joint USAF/NASA follow-on flight test program which had been slated to begin on June 15, 1966. But due to the tragic mid-air collision that particular flight test program didn't get off the ground until November 3.

XB-70A-2 lies demolished in California's Mojave Desert after the tragic mid-air collision between it and an F-104 a short time before.

Rockwell

Al White's escape module after impact about ten miles north of XB-70A-2's crash area. White survived the mid-air tragedy because he successfully encapsulated himself and ejected before it was too late. During his ejection sequence, White's right arm jammed in between his ejection hand grip and the edge of the upper escape capsule door, when he forcibly pulled his arm inside, he pulled his arm out from its shoulder socket. He received additional back and internal injuries when his capsule hit ground at an estimated 43 Gs force. Note that his impact bladder door is shut, that it didn't open and inflate. It was for this reason that his capsule hit so hard.   Rockwell

All that was left of Carl Cross' escape module after the tragic mid-air collision between his aircraft, XB-70A-2, and an F-104 on 8 June 1966. The reason he didn't eject is unclear, but Cross' failure to escape probably resulted from his failure to encapsulate and eject before longitudinal G-forces built up to the point where he was incapacitated.   Rockwell

In early 1966, NASA allocated $10 million for B-70 flight test research. This action was followed in late spring by a second effort on NASA's part to establish an enlarged flight research program, designed to last 18 months. To do this, NASA allocated another $40 million. This high cost was directly attributed to in-

stallation of sophisticated, computerized instrumentation within XB-70A-2's fuselage and weapons bay. More than a thousand sensors were installed to register data vital to development of future supersonic aircraft. Unfortunately, this was all lost in the mid-air collision.

The joint USAF/NAA flight test program, which had been directed by the USAF System Command's Aeronautical Systems at Wright-Patterson AFB, Ohio, and managed by North American Aviation, Inc., had been completed in early June, and everyone was gearing up for the joint USAF/NASA flight test program. But the unfortunate mid-air tragedy changed things, the program was put aside when the Air Force extended the USAF/NAA flight test program until July 5, 1966, to evaluate the feasibility of entering the USAF/NASA phase with XB-70A-1 which had been grounded on May 9 for systems updating. Serious doubts arose over the ability of XB-70A-1 to accomplish the ambitious goals planned for the USAF/NASA flight test program. These doubts persisted and finally forced the USAF to cancel further B-70 research. It was then up to NASA alone. NASA decided to install its test equipment in XB-70A-1 while it was grounded.

The cold, hard fact that the tragic mid-air collision had occurred during a portion of a military flight test in which photographs were being taken for a private firm had a serious impact on Congress. Two boards were appointed to investigate the crash. A memorandum from Secretary of the Air Force Harold Brown to Secretary of Defense Robert S. McNamara contained the board's findings. Blame was placed on three USAF colonels— Col. Cate, Col. Cotton, and Col. Smith. Col. Smith was a public information officer who had failed to notify USAF Systems Command of the public relations photography session. And a Mr. McCollum, who was at Edwards the day prior to the tragedy, who had been briefed on the photo-taking session, was reprimanded for not using his authority to stop the flight. Col. Cate was transferred to other duties; Col. Cotton was reprimanded.

During updating and systems installation, XB-70A number one was retrofitted with one expensive system that improved its emergency escape capsules. This retrofit cost over $2 million. In addition, the "trick" computerized AICS like the one installed in ship number 2, thereby eliminating its troublesome manual air induction control system. Grounding was lifted on November 1, 1966, and XB-70A-1 was prepared for further flight testing.

This particular B-70 flight test phase was to evaluate controlled sonic boom experiments

among other tests such as point-to-point maneuvers associated with anticipated SST flight envelopes. Because both the Air Force and NASA had equally allocated funds for Phase II, Part II, it remained a joint USAF/NASA venture for a time; directed by NASA, managed by the USAF, using Edwards' facilities. Eleven USAF/NASA flight tests were flown before the Air Force finally bowed out. Then NASA took over as the sole B-70 sponsor.

The first NASA flight occurred on April 25, 1967. Joe Cotton served as pilot and Fitz Fulton was copilot. Twenty-three flight tests were performed by the NASA organization. The highest speed attained during this phase was Mach 2.55 at 67,000 ft.

Between January 31 and April 25, 1967, additional instrumentation designed to measure structural response to gusts, stability and control, boundary layer noise, and SST simulation was installed.

Earlier, NASA had opted for SST flight research between the speeds of M2.5 and 3.0 but, as noted previously, continued problems with skin losses during high mach flight placed a Mach 2.5 maximum on XB-70A-1 for safety. Therefore, NASA was forced to restrict their high speed flights to M2.5, and M2.55 was reached twice.

Prior to the tragic loss of XB-70A-2, it had become a flying laboratory and highly sophisticated test vehicle for the proposed Boeing 733 SST. The government and private researchers embarked on a major sonic boom test program at Edwards in an effort to accurately forecast psychological reaction and structural damage associated with sonic booms from supersonic transports. This National Sonic Boom Program (NSBP), as it was called, was set up by President Johnson's Office of Science and Technology, and consisted of three principal participants: the USAF, the NASA, and the Stanford Research Institute.

A sonic boom is created when there is a pressure change on the ground across a shock wave produced by the passage of a supersonic airplane overhead. The sound and destruction can be both disturbing and costly to persons on the ground, thus it became necessary to investigate sonic booms. The B-70 was selected to perform sonic boom tests because it more nearly approximated Boeing's SST size than smaller aircraft such as Convair's B-58 or Lockheed's F-104 as used previously. B-70 was the only aircraft capable of approximating the SST because its weight and size had a marked affect on sonic boom signatures. Even

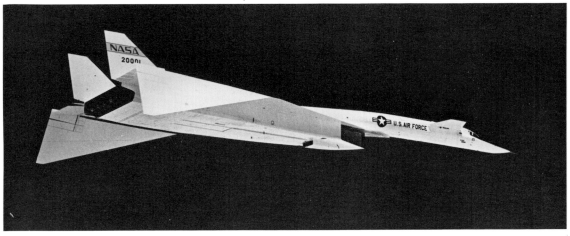

XB-70A-1 shown inflight with its v-g wingtips lowered fulldown to 65 degrees. This was the first time that XB-70A-1 flew under NASA's sponsorship. This flight occurred on April 25, 1967, and lasted 1 hour, 7 minutes.   *NASA via Jackson*

XB-70A-1 rolls to a stop at Edwards, parabrake chutes deployed. Note elevons, canard flaps deflected downward. Three 28-foot diameter parachutes were housed in compartment atop aft fuselage between vertical tails.   *Rockwell*

First NASA XB-70A flight on 25 April 1967. Twenty-two additional NASA flights were flown, the last occurred on 4 February 1969, when XB-70A-1 was retired to the Air Force Museum.   *NASA*

though over pressures of equal peak magnitudes could be obtained with F-104s and B-58s, the duration of the boom itself varied with each aircraft as do the shape of the shock waves themselves and the forces involved. It was felt that B-70 aircraft would provide longer-duration shock wave shape and force during sonic booms generated by them, that more accurate data would be obtained.

The NSBP began on June 6, 1966. XB-70A-2 performed this initial sonic boom test, reaching M3.05 at 72,000 feet. The second NSBP test occurred on June 8 as scheduled, however, it was followed by the mid-air collision soon afterward. Testing didn't resume until November 3, 1966, when XB-70A-1 entered

XB-70A-1 rotating for its last time on February 4, 1969, as it heads for Wright-Patterson AFB, Ohio, where it was retired to the Air Force Museum. It was its 83rd and last flight. Note inside elevon and canard flap deflection.   Rockwell

Shown boarding XB-70A-1 for the last time are Fitz Fulton and Ted Sturmthal. Pilot Fulton and copilot Sturmthal departed Edwards AFB at 10:57 a.m. on 4 February 1969 and arrived at the Air Force Museum at Wright-Patterson AFB at 2:15 p.m. Original XB-70A flight test plans called for each ship to be flown 180 hours, however, XB-70A-1's log book closed showing 160 hours 18 minutes; XB-70A-2 perished with a total flight time of 92 hours 22 minutes. Thus both aircraft accumulated a total flight time of 252 hours 4 minutes. Sturmthal is behind Fulton.   Rockwell

the NSBP. Some 250 sonic boom tests were planned, mostly at over pressures of 1.5 to 3.0 pounds per square foot, but some 4.0 psf booms were figured into the test program. Over pressure is about equal to the square root of an aircraft's weight. Therefore, a 300,000 pound SST, cruising at M2.7 at 65,000 feet, was expected to generate an over pressure of 2.0 psf. On one test, where XB-70A-1 weighed 423,000 pounds while traveling M1.22 at 27,000 feet, it caused an over pressure of 3.15 psf. A B-58 just behind it, weighing 120,000 pounds, generated 2.87 psf. It was determined that despite the 303,000 pound difference in weight, with only 0.28 psf over pressure dif-

ference, that the near field affect (somewhat shaky pressure signature) had reduced the B-70's sonic boom intensity.

It was found that sonic booms are affected by many factors: temperature inversions, mach number at altitude fluctuations, unparalled shock waves, and variations in aircraft weight and size. Other factors are still being investigated and some day science may find a way to cope with them.

Retirement

The final NASA flight test was originally scheduled for an 8:00 a.m. departure on January 22, 1969, but it was delayed until 4 February. Then at 10:57 a.m., the only existing B-70 rotated and climbed away from what had been its home for some five years—Edwards AFB, California. Its destination: Wright-Patterson AFB, Ohio, and the Air Force Museum.

The B-70 has been called everything from "a banana pulling an orange crate" to the great white bird. It was a majestic airplane and its pilots respected it. Two of its pilots, Fitz Fulton and Ted Sturmthal, commanded it on the final flight to the Air Force Museum. And even on the final flight it recorded research data; ILAF and shaker vane information was gathered during its 3 hour, 18 minute trip to Wright-Patterson AFB. The 1880 statute mile trip was flown at M0.91 subsonic cruise at 33,000 feet. No supersonic dash occurred. Prior to its final landing it made a farewell pass over the field. Then at 2:15 p.m. it touched the runway, popped its three chutes, rolled out the momentum and stopped.

In the race to build an American SST, North American investigated several SST designs based upon its XB-70 M3 bomber.
Rockwell

Pilot Fulton turned over the keys and log book to the Air Force Museum's curator. He slowly turned his back and walked to the awaiting crew van, he didn't look back. And if he had sneaked a look back he wouldn't have told anyone.

Valkyrie 1 had carried on proudly since its sister ship had perished. It was its 83rd flight and its log book was closed showing a total flight time of 160 hours, 18 minutes.

Considering the total cost of the B-70 program, which has been reported as $1.5 billion, it cost about $11.6 million per flight—that is, considering both aircraft and a total of 129 flight tests between them. It was this staggering fact that may have prompted Sturmthal to say, "I'd do anything to keep the B-70 in the air, except pay for it myself."

XB-70A-1 upon arrival at Wright-Patterson AFB, Ohio, where it was turned over to the Air Force Museum. Shown exiting are Fitzhugh L. Fulton, Jr., pilot, and Emil (Ted) Sturmthal, copilot. During an interview with the attending press afterwards copilot Sturmthal said, "I'd do anything to keep the B-70 in the air, except pay for it myself."
Air Force Museum

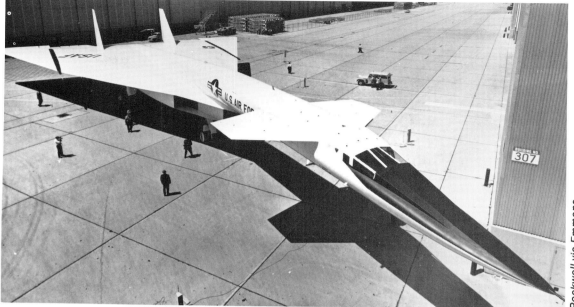

Appendices

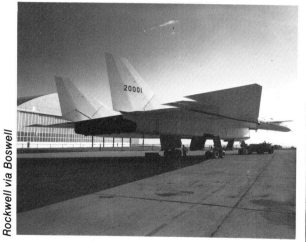

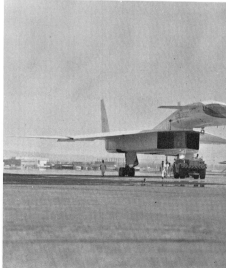

APPENDIX A: CONTRACT GENEALOGY

December 9, 1955
   Model NA-239, USAF/SAC bomber, contract number AF-31801, Los Angeles Division. Engineering design proposal and mock-up for XB-70A and XB-70L (previously Weapons System 110A and 110L). Nuclear-powered WS-110L cancelled per MCPHBF-6-6-E on June 7, 1956.

January 2, 1958
   Model NA-259, USAF B-70, contract number AF-36599. XB-70A Phase I. Follow-on program to NA-239.

December 31, 1958
   Model NA-264, USAF, contract number AF-38669. XB-70A Phase II, Part I. Follow-on program to NA-259.

July 27, 1959
   Model NA-267, USAF, same contract as above. XB-70A Phase II, Part II redirection. Follow-on program to NA-264.

September 21, 1960
   Model NA-274, USAF YB-70B, contract number AF-42058. A single YB-70B prototype weapon system development. Follow-on program to NA-267, serial number 62-0208

April 10, 1961
   Model NA-278, USAF, contract number AF-42058. Order for two XB-70A prototype aircraft, serial numbers 62-0001 and 62-0207. Follow-on program to NA-267. YB-70B cancelled March 5, 1964.

January 18, 1962
   Model NA-281, USAF, contract number AF-12395, factory serial number 281-1, AF serial number 62-0001. Flight test program.

March 13, 1963
   Model NA-286, USAF, contract number AF-42058. Cost accumulation order, closed at termination of XB-70A number 3, Model NA-278.

March 5, 1964
   Model NA-274 YB-70B cancelled, see 9/21/60.

January 24, 1966
   Model NA-303, USAF/ASD, contract number AF33(657)-15871, factory serial number 281-1, AF serial number 62-0001. Flight test program.

March 17, 1967
   Model NA-315, NASA, contract number NAS4-1175, factory serial number 281-1, AF serial number 62-0001. NASA flight test program; XB-70 flight research.

B-70 technologies made creation of an SST possible. Russia's SST flew in December 1968 while the British/French Concorde SST flew in February 1969. Boeing's proposed SST is illustrated here. *Boeing*

APPENDIX B: SPECIFICATIONS

Manufacturer
    North American Aviation, Inc. (now Rockwell International)
Model Number(s)
    NA-278 (XB-70A); NA-274 for cancelled YB-70B
Designation(s)
    XB-70A
Popular Name
    Valkyrie
Service(s)
    U. S. Air Force Strategic Air Command, NASA
Primary Mission
    Intercontinental Strategic Bomber
Crew
    Two (flight test program); Four (operational)
Roll-out
    XB-70A-1, May 11, 1964; XB-70A-2, May 29, 1965
First Flight
    XB-70A-1, September 21, 1964; XB-70A-2, July 17, 1965
Number Built
    Two
Serial Number(s)
    XB-70A-1, 62-0001; XB-70A-2, 62-0207; Cancelled YB-70B, 62-0208
Length
    189.0 feet (196.0 ft. with nose probe)
Height
    30.0 feet
Wing Span
    105.0 feet
Wing Area
    6,297.15 square feet
Gross Weight
    550,000-plus pounds
Speed
    Mach 3.0-plus (2,000-plus mph); M3.08 attained
Range
    7,600 nautical miles, unrefueled
Ceiling
    70,000 to 80,000 feet; 74,000 feet attained
Power Plants
    Six General Electric YJ93-GE-3 afterburning turbojets of 30,000 pounds static sea-level
    thrust each
Armament
    None
Payload
    50,000 pounds of either nuclear or conventional weapons

Remarks
    XB-70A-2 was lost in a mid-air collision June 8, 1966; XB-70A-1 was retired to the Air Force
    Museum February 4, 1969; 129 flight tests were accomplished by both aircraft at pro-
    gram's completion.

APPENDIX C: B-70 FLIGHT LOG & SUMMARY

NO.	DATE	FLIGHT NUMBER	PILOT/COPILOT	MACH/MPH	ALT(ft)	HR MIN	NOTES
1	9-21-64	1-1	White/Cotton	0.50/360	16,000	1 07	first flight #1
2	10-5-64	1-2	White/Cotton	0.85/600	28,000	0 55	
(3)	10-12-64	1-3	White/Cotton	1.11/725	35,400	1 35	supersonic for 15 minutes, landed at Palmdale
4	10-24-64	1-4	White/Cotton	1.42/945	46,300	1 25	
5	2-16-65	1-5	White/Cotton	1.60/1060	45,000	1 10	
6	2-25-65	1-6	White/Fulton	0.97/655	35,000	0 53	
7	3-4-65	1-7	White/Fulton	1.85/1200	50,200	1 37	
(8)	3-24-65	1-8	White/Shepard	2.14/1365	56,100	1 40	first double-sonic flight
9	4-2-65	1-9	White/Cotton	0.95/630	34,500	0 54	
10	4-20-65	1-10	White/Cotton	2.30/1485	58,500	1 42	
11	4-28-65	1-11	White/Shepard	2.45/1570	65,300	1 43	
12	5-7-65	1-12	White/Fulton	2.60/1690	65,000	1 25	
13	6-16-65	1-13	White/Cotton	2.60/1700	65,000	1 37	
14	7-1-65	1-14	White/Shepard	2.85/1900	68,000	1 44	
(15)	7-17-65	2-1	White/Cotton	1.41/935	42,000	1 13	first flight #2
16	7-27-65	1-15	White/Fulton	2.82/1900	66,000	1 43	
17	8-10-65	2-2	Cotton/White	1.45/950	41,000	1 27	
18	8-18-65	2-3	Shepard/White	1.45/950	46,000	1 58	
19	8-20-65	2-4	Fulton/White	1.44/950	42,000	2 04	
20	9-17-65	2-5	White/Fulton	1.83/1200	50,500	1 55	
21	9-22-65	1-16	White/Cotton	2.83/1900	67,000	1 57	
22	9-29-65	2-6	White/Shepard	2.23/1460	54,000	1 44	
23	10-5-65	2-7	White/Shepard	2.30/1520	55,000	1 40	
24	10-11-65	2-8	White/Shepard	2.34/1550	57,500	1 55	
(25)	10-14-65	1-17	White/Cotton	3.02/2000	70,000	1 47	first triple-sonic flight
26	10-16-65	2-9	White/Fulton	2.43/1600	59,500	1 43	
27	10-26-65	2-10	White/Fulton	2.46/1620	59,000	2 07	
28	11-2-65	2-11	White/Cotton	2.45/1610	59,000	1 54	
29	11-4-65	1-18	Fulton/White	1.86/1200	46,000	2 04	
30	11-8-65	1-19	Cotton/White	1.89/1210	45,500	2 23	
31	11-12-65	1-20	Shepard/White	1.84/1190	46,000	2 25	
32	11-18-65	1-21	Cotton/Shepard	1.88/1210	47,000	2 02	
33	11-29-65	2-12	White/Fulton	0.53/370	15,200	2 19	
34	11-30-65	1-22	Fulton/White	2.34/1490	56,000	1 59	
35	12-1-65	2-13	White/Fulton	2.67/1765	64,000	2 02	
36	12-2-65	1-23	Cotton/White	2.46/1620	60,000	1 51	
37	12-3-65	2-14	White/Cotton	2.87/1900	69,000	1 55	
38	12-7-65	1-24	Shepard/Fulton	2.45/1600	62,000	2 26	
39	12-10-65	1-25	Fulton/Shepard	1.82/1200	50,700	2 18	
40	12-11-65	2-15	White/Shepard	2.94/1940	70,600	2 03	
41	12-14-65	1-26	Shepard/Fulton	0.95/650	20,000	2 10	
42	12-20-65	1-27	Cotton/White	1.78/1190	42,000	1 58	
43	12-21-65	2-16	White/Cotton	2.95/1945	72,000	1 49	
44	12-22-65	1-28	Shepard/Cotton	1.42/950	34,000	2 35	
(45)	1-3-66	2-17	White/Cotton	3.05/2010	72,000	1 52	first triple-sonic flight #2
46	1-3-66	1-29	Fulton/Shepard	0.94/655	26,000	2 41	both, same day. longest flight.
(47)	1-6-66	1-30	Shepard/Fulton	0.94/655	33,000	3 40	
48	1-11-66	1-31	Fulton/Shepard	1.85/1220	46,000	1 35	
49	1-11-66	1-32	Cotton/White	0.95/650	27,000	0 58	
50	1-12-66	2-18	White/Cotton	3.06/2020	72,000	1 48	

NO.	DATE	FLIGHT NUMBER	PILOT/COPILOT	MACH/MPH	ALT(ft)	HR MIN	NOTES
51	1-15-66	1-33	Fulton/White	1.85/1220	47,000	1 27	
52	2-7-66	2-19	Shepard/ Cotton	1.44/960	42,000	2 11	
53	2-9-66	2-20	White/Cotton	3.04/2000	70,800	1 49	
54	2-16-66	2-21	White/Cotton	1.10/720	32,000	3 06	
55	2-17-66	2-22	White/Cotton	3.04/2000	73,000	1 47	
56	2-26-66	1-34	Shepard/Fulton	0.92/650	20,000	2 22	
57	3-3-66	1-35	Fulton/Shepard	0.55/350	15,000	2 42	
58	3-4-66	1-36	Fulton/Shepard	2.02/1330	56,000	2 27	
59	3-7-66	1-37	Shepard/ Cotton	2.22/1450	57,000	2 19	
60	3-10-66	2-23	White/Fulton	2.76/1820	67,000	1 51	
61	3-15-66	2-24	White/Fulton	2.85/1880	69,500	1 59	
62	3-17-66	2-25	Fulton/White	2.85/1880	70,350	1 52	
(63)	3-19-66	2-26	White/Shepard	2.93/1930	74,000	1 57	highest flight.
64	3-23-66	1-38	Cotton/ Shepard	0.97/660	32,000	2 11	
65	3-24-66	2-27	Fulton/White	2.71/1600	64,000	1 32	landed Carswell AFB.
66	3-24-66	1-39	Shepard/ Cotton	2.42/1600	60,000	2 00	
67	3-26-66	2-28	Cotton/White	0.94/650	36,000	3 09	T.O. Carswell AFB, landed Edwards AFB.
68	3-28-66	1-40	Shepard/ Cotton	2.43/1600	65,000	1 41	
69	3-29-66	2-29	Shepard/White	1.65/1090	48,000	1 51	
70	3-31-66	2-30	Shepard/White	2.95/1950	72,000	2 10	
71	4-1-66	1-41	White/Fulton	2.45/1620	58,800	2 07	
72	4-4-66	2-31	Cotton/White	2.95/1940	73,000	1 57	
73	4-5-66	1-42	Fulton/Shepard	2.43/1600	61,000	2 01	
74	4-8-66	2-32	Fulton/White	3.07/2000	73,000	2 05	
(75)	4-12-66	2-33	White/Cotton	3.08/2000	72,800	1 49	fastest flight.
76	4-13-66	1-43	Shepard/ Cotton	2.60/1700	62,500	2 03	
77	4-16-66	2-34	White/Cotton	3.03/2000	71,000	2 01	
78	4-19-66	1-44	Shepard/Fulton	0.58/270k	17,000	2 12	
79	4-21-66	1-45	Shepard/Fulton	2.42/1600	61,000	2 02	
80	4-23-66	2-35	White/Cotton	2.73/1800	66,000	2 01	
81	4-25-66	1-46	Fulton/Shepard	2.55/1680	63,000	2 07	
82	4-26-66	2-36	Fulton/Cotton	2.65/1760	65,500	2 05	
83	4-27-66	1-47	White/Fulton	1.50/1010	31,000	2 41	
84	4-30-66	2-37	White/Cotton	/285k	16,000	2 16	
85	5-3-66	1-48	White/Fulton	/275k	23,000	1 22	
86	5-9-66	1-49	White/Fulton	/270k	15,000	2 16	
87	5-16-66	2-38	White/Cotton	2.73/1800	65,000	2 09	
88	5-19-66	2-39	White/Cotton	3.06/2000	72,500	1 59	
89	5-22-66	2-40	Fulton/Cotton	1.51/960	36,500	2 22	
90	5-25-66	2-41	Shepard/ Cotton	1.63/1065	42,000	2 23	
91	5-27-66	2-42	Shepard/ Cotton	2.53/1640	62,000	2 08	
92	5-31-66	2-43	Shepard/Fulton	2.25/1455	57,000	2 02	
93	6-4-66	2-44	Shepard/ Cotton	2.93/1930	70,000	2 05	
94	6-6-66	2-45	Shepard/ Cotton	3.05/2000	72,000	2 00	

NO.	DATE	FLIGHT NUMBER	PILOT/COPILOT	MACH/MPH	ALT(ft)	HR MIN	NOTES
(95)	6-8-66	2-46	White/Cross	1.41/940	32,000	2 13	F-104 & XB-70-2 mid-air collision, fatal to Cross and Walker.
96	11-3-66	1-50	Cotton/Fulton	2.10/	60,000	2 00	
97	11-10-66	1-51	Fulton/Cotton	2.52/	60,000	1 39	
98	11-23-66	1-52	Shepard/Cotton	2.51/	61,000	1 38	
99	12-12-66	1-53	Fulton/Shepard	2.52/	60,000	1 57	
100	12- -66	1-54	Shepard/Fulton	2.55/	60,300	1 54	
101	12-20-66	1-55	Cotton/Shepard	2.53/	60,800	1 45	
102	1-4-67	1-56	Fulton/Shepard	2.53/	60,400	1 44	
103	1-	1-57	Cotton/Fulton	2.57/	61,000	1 46	
104	1-17-67	1-58	Cotton/Shepard	2.56/	60,200	1 42	
105	1- -67	1-59	Fulton/Shepard	1.40/	35,000	1 32	
106	1-31-67	1-60	Fulton/Cotton	1.40/	37,000	1 32	
(107)	4-25-67	1-61	Cotton/Fulton	/265k	17,000	1 07	first NASA flight.
108	5-12-67	1-62	Fulton/Cotton	/275k	16,500	2 17	
109	6-2-67	1-63	Cotton/Shepard	1.43/	42,000	2 23	
110	6-22-67	1-64	Fulton/Mallick	1.83/	54,000	1 54	
111	8-10-67	1-65	Cotton/Sturmthal	0.92/	15,500	2 27	
112	8-24-67	1-66	Fulton/Mallick	2.24/	57,700	1 52	
113	9-8-67	1-67	Cotton/Sturmthal	2.3/	61,000	1 50	
114	10-11-67	1-68	Fulton/Mallick	2.43/	58,000	1 39	
115	11-2-67	1-69	Cotton/Sturmthal	2.55/	64,000	1 56	
116	1-12-68	1-70	Fulton/Mallick	2.55/	67,000	1 54	
117	2-13-68	1-71	Mallick/Cotton	1.18/	41,000	2 43	
118	2-28-68	1-72	Fulton/Sturmthal	/255k	18,500	1 51	
119	3-21-68	1-73	Cotton/Fulton	/270k	15,500	2 32	
120	6-11-68	1-74	Mallick/Fulton	unk.	unk.	1 09	
121	6-28-68	1-75	Sturmthal/Cotton	unk.	unk.	2 37	
122	7-19-68	1-76	Mallick/Fulton	unk.	unk.	1 53	
123	8-16-68	1-77	Fulton/Sturmthal	2.47/	63,000	1 55	
124	9-10-68	1-78	Mallick/Fulton	unk.	unk.	1 45	
125	10-18-68	1-79	Fulton/Sturmthal	2.18/	52,000	1 53	
126	11-1-68	1-80	Sturmthal/Fulton	unk.	unk.	2 06	
127	12-3-68	1-81	Mallick/Fulton	unk.	unk.	1 58	
128	12-17-68	1-82	Fulton/Sturmthal	unk.	unk.	2 42	
(129)	2-4-69	1-83	Fulton/Sturmthal	0.91/	33,000	3 18	final flight, landed at Dayton, Ohio W-P AFB.

APPENDIX C: B-70 FLIGHT TEST LOG AND SUMMARY

XB-70 pilots in order of chronological flight and number of flights as pilot and copilot.

1. Alvin S. White, North American, retired: 49 as pilot, 18 as copilot.
2. Colonel Joseph F. Cotton, USAF: 19 as pilot, 43 as copilot.
3. Van H. Shepard, North American, retired: 23 as pilot, 23 as copilot.
4. Fitzhugh L. Fulton, Jr., USAF-NASA: 31 as pilot, 32 as copilot.
5. Major Carl S. Cross, USAF: 1 as copilot.[1]
6. Donald L. Mallick, NASA: 4 as pilot, 5 as copilot.
7. Emil (Ted) Sturmthal, USAF: 3 as pilot, 7 as copilot.

First Flight: September 21, 1964; White and Cotton.

Final Flight: February 4, 1969; Fulton and Sturmthal.

Fastest Flight: April 12, 1966, Mach 3.08; White and Cotton.

Highest Flight: March 19, 1966, 74,000 feet; White and Shepard.

Total Flight Time (both aircraft): 252 hours, 38 minutes.

Total Flight Time:

	Subsonic	Supersonic	Doublesonic	Triplesonic
(Hrs, Mins)	145:28	55:50	49:32	1:48

Note 1: Major Carl S. Cross lost his life June 8, 1966, while copiloting XB-70 number 2. He had been assigned to replace Fulton on the B-70 pilot's roster.

XB-70A-1's 61st flight on April 25, 1967. This was the 1st NASA-sponsored test flight; Joe Cotton served as pilot and Fitz Fulton was copilot. NASA flew another 22 flights before B-70's flight test program was terminated.

NASA via Jackson

First XB-70A flight crew. Left to right are Fitz Fulton, Van Shepard, Joe Cotton, and Al White. Three other pilots flew XB-70 aircraft later: Ted Sturmthal, Carl Cross, and Don Mallick. Joe Walker had been assigned to fly the aircraft, but was killed in a mid-air collision with one before he had a chance to fly in one. Rockwell

NASA XB-70A test pilots Fitzhugh L. Fulton (left) and Donald L Mallick (right) congratulated each other following a successful flight June 22, 1967. It was the first time up in the B-70 for Mallick; a flight which lasted one hour and 54 minutes.

NASA

Al White following flight of XB-70A-2 from Edwards AFB, California, to Carswell AFB, Texas, on March 24, 1966. It only took one hour and 32 minutes to make the journey; M2.71 at 64,000 was achieved.

Rockwell

Left to right are Charlie Bock, Jr. Dick Abrams and Ted Sturmthal. Sturmthal, after going M2-plus in a B-1A became the only pilot to exceed M2 in two different bomber types; he exceeded M2 in B-70 aircraft on four occasions.

Rockwell via Holland

XB-70A-2's 5 degree wing dihedral shows up well in this aft view. The requirement for the wing dihedral was determined during wind tunnel investigations after production was begun. The design change came during manufacture. The dihedral offered improved highspeed stability.   *Rockwell*

Note that lower radome is black on XB-70A-2; XB-70A-1's remained white throughout its career.
Rockwell

XB-70 WHEELS ARE WIDER THAN ROAD—A tow crew member guides tow truck pulling the XB-70 onto highway just outside Wright-Patterson AFB, Ohio, gate. The large aircraft's wide landing gear presented a unique towing problem, but with a few innovations the crew completed their mission.   *U.S. Air Force*

XB-70A-1 at Wright Patterson AFB, Ohio. Plane was flown there to be part of the U.S. Air Force Museum dis plays February 4, 1969, it was its 83rd flight.   *Air Force Museum*

This photograph of the XB-70 was taken on the day that it arrived at Wright-Patterson AFB, February 4, 1969. This particular angle shows how the B-70 acquired the "Hooded Cobra" nickname; just one of many given to Valkyrie.   *Air Force Museum photo*

ANNOTATED BIBLIOGRAPHY

Aviation Week & Space Technology, McGraw-Hill, New York, N.Y.
    Published weekly, this magazine is one of the best, if not the best, sources for current aircraft information. For past reference materials it cannot be overlooked. This magazine always presents excellent data pertaining to the world's aircraft, missiles and spacecraft.

Jane's all the World's Aircraft, McGraw-Hill, New York, N.Y., 1966.
    The most respected of all reference books. Good details of the North American XB-70 Valkyrie are presented in this particular volume. An annual since 1909, this publication may be considered to be the Bible of aviation.

Emmons, Douglas L. *The B-70 Valkyrie Story.* The United States Air Force Museum, 1980.
    An excellent run-down on the B-70, written for presentation by the Air Force Museum. This publication covers the growth and mission of the B-70 very well indeed.

Gunston, Bill. *Bombers of the West.* Charles Scribner's Sons, New York, N.Y. 1973.
    Contains a chapter which deals with the B-70, which places the aircraft in the military-political arena, comparing it to other manned bomber types. A good overview of the B-70 program.

Miles, Marvin. *The "Thump" of Disaster: Test Pilot Recalls 1966 Crash of the B-70 Bomber.* The Los Angeles Times, 1966.
    Excellent account of test pilot Alvin White's tragedy and the loss of two friends. An aerospace writer for the L.A. Times, Miles has contributed greatly to aerospace related events. This article is just one of those contributions.

Foxworth, Thomas G. *North American XB-70; Half Airplane—Half Spacecraft.* Part 1 and 2, Historical Aviation Album; Volume 7, 1969 and Volume 8, 1970. Matt, Paul R., Publisher, Temple City, California.
    Accurate, detailed two-part article dealing with the B-70. Historical Aviation Album always presents excellent data pertaining to selected historical aircraft as well as super detailed scale drawings of those craft. An excellent source for the serious aviation buff or historian.

Pace, Stephen L. *The Great White Bird.* Air Classics Quarterly Review, Challenge Publications, Canoga Park, California; Volume 4/Number 3; Fall 1977.
    This quarterly magazine offers good data on the various aircraft of the world. It's a good start for the B-70 enthusiast.

Pike, Iian. *B-70: State-of-the-Art-Improver.* Flight International, June 25 and July 2, 1964.
    Highly technical two-part magazine article dealing with the B-70 before it flew. Great source for continued research into this airplane.

Noland, Dave. *XB-70 Greatest of Them All?* World's Great Aircraft, 1972.
    Short, concise article on the B-70; well written and to the point.

Mansfield, Harold. *"Vision: The Story of Boeing.* Duell, Sloan and Pearce, New York, N.Y. 1966.
    Provides a look at Boeing's involvement in the B-70 program; explains why Boeing lost the competition to North American. Excellent, unbiased overview.

U. S. Air Force ROTC Air University. *Fundamentals of Aerospace Weapon Systems.* U. S. Government Printing Office, 1961.
    Deals with most aspects of American aerospace weapon systems including the B-70 as proposed in 1961.

Stinton, Darrol. *The Anatomy of the Aeroplane.* American Elsevier Publishing Company, Inc., New York, N.Y., 1966.
    Good reference book dealing with aerodynamics which gives an excellent account of B-70's "compression lift."

Schleicher, Richard L., Sc. D. *Structural Design Of The XB-70.* North American Aviation, Inc., 1967.
    Twenty-five page manual representing a paper which Dr. Schleicher presented to the Institute of Aeronautical Sciences in 1967. Very factual and in-depth. Unfortunately, this particular publication is not available to the general public.

Slawsky, Richard. *XB-70 Pilots Describe the World of Mach 3.* Airline Management and Marketing Magazine, Part 1 and 2, March and April 1967.

> Great two-part feature article interviewing several B-70 test pilots. It provides their respective insight to the B-70 flight test program. A must for the serious B-70 student.

Wagner, Ray. *American Combat Planes.* Hanover House, Garden City, New York, Third Edition, 1981.

> This edition of American Combat Planes covers the B-70, as a bomber and as a test vehicle. Good reading, good knowledge.

Astrophile Supplement, NASA Flight Research Center, XB-70 Research Aircraft, Flight Test Chronology. pp 79–82.

> Complete B-70 flight test chronology from flight 1 to 129.

XB-70A Number 1 and 2 Flight Hours Log and Flight Summary, Prepared by Engineering Flight Test, North American Aviation, Inc., July 1, 1966. pp 1–20.

> Complete run-down of all B-70 flight tests, highlighting B-70 performances.

Jones, Lloyd S. *U. S. Bombers: 1928 to 1980s.* Aero Publishers, Inc., Fallbrook, California, Second Edition, 1980.

> Complete geneology of the American bomber plane from the Keystone XB-1 of 1928 to the Rockwell B-1 of the 1980 decade. Good source for B-70 data.

Gentle, E. J. and Reithmaier, L. W. *Aviation & Space Dictionary.* Aero Publishers, Inc., Fallbrook, California, Sixth Edition, 1980.

> An essential learning tool for aviation buffs and historians alike. This particular publication provided definitions for B-70 terminologies.

XB-70A-1 was moved six miles down Route 444 to its final home, the new Air Force Museum near Dayton, Ohio, during 24-25 October 1970. Note house mover.   *Air Force Museum via Worman*

DETAIL & SCALE SERIES . . .

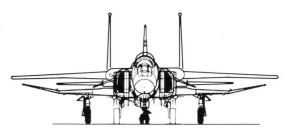

The F-15 Eagle in Detail & Scale

The Detail & Scale Series of publications is unique in aviation literature. Instead of an emphasis on history, the attention is focused on many physical details of the aircraft such as cockpit interiors, radar and avionics installations, armament, landing gear, wheel wells, and ejection seats. These details are covered in close-up photography and line drawings. The Detail & Scale Series is detailed, technical and accurate.

Like the preceding D & S volumes, **Volume 14, The F-15 Eagle** contains 5-view drawings, technical data and tables, performance data, mission profiles, historical development summaries, armament and ordnance coverage, modelers kit review section, and scads of detailed photos.

ISBN 0-8168-5028-3   72 pages   paper $7.95

COLORS & MARKINGS SERIES . . .

The F-106 Delta Dart in Colors & Markings

The Colors & Markings Series has been designed to provide an ongoing affordable series of publications covering the paint schemes, squadron markings, special insignias, and nose art carried by many of the most important aircraft in aviation history.

The first volume in the new Colors & Markings Series is the most complete reference ever published on the colors and unit markings carried by the **F-106 Delta Dart**.

It details each unit that flew the "Six," when it received the F-106, and when it deactivated, transitioned to a new aircraft, or was redesignated, and the dates of each event. Almost two-hundred photographs, some never before published, 16 pages in full color.

ISBN 0-8168-4525-5   64 pages paper $9.95